Application Development with Qt Creator

Second Edition

Design and build dazzling cross-platform applications using Qt and Qt Quick

Ray Rischpater

[PACKT] open source *
PUBLISHING
community experience distilled

BIRMINGHAM - MUMBAI

Application Development with Qt Creator
Second Edition

First published: November 2013

Second edition: November 2014

Production reference: 1221114

Published by Packt Publishing Ltd.
Livery Place
35 Livery Street
Birmingham B3 2PB, UK.

ISBN 978-1-78439-867-5

www.packtpub.com

Credits

Author

Ray Rischpater

Reviewers

Lee Zhi Eng

Andrea Flesca

Niels Holst

Sudhendu Kumar

Commissioning Editor

Usha Iyer

Acquisition Editor

Llewellyn Rozario

Content Development Editor

Ritika Singh

Technical Editors

Venu Manthena

Edwin Moses

Copy Editors

Dipti Kapadia

Deepa Nambiar

Project Coordinator

Aboli Ambardekar

Proofreaders

Ting Baker

Simran Bhogal

Paul Hindle

Steve Maguire

Indexers

Monica Ajmera Mehta

Rekha Nair

Graphics

Abhinash Sahu

Production Coordinators

Pooja Chiplunkar

Alwin Roy

Cover Work

Alwin Roy

About the Author

Ray Rischpater is an engineer and author, with over 20 years of experience in writing about mobile computing platforms and developing for them.

During this time, he has participated in the development of Internet technologies and custom applications for Java ME, Qualcomm Brew™, Apple iPhone, Google Android, Palm OS, Newton, and Magic Cap, as well as several proprietary platforms. Presently, he's employed as a Senior Engineer at Microsoft in Mountain View, and he works on mapping and data visualization.

When he is not writing for software development or about it, he enjoys hiking and photography with his family and friends in and around the San Lorenzo Valley in Central California. Whenever he's able to, he provides a public service through amateur radio as the licensed Amateur Extra station KF6GPE.

Among the books that he has written are *Microsoft Mapping*, with Carmen Au, *Apress, 2013* and *Beginning Java ME Platform, Apress, 2008*. Ray also irregularly blogs at `http//www.lothlorien.com/kf6gpe`.

He holds a Bachelor's degree in Pure Mathematics from the University of California, Santa Cruz, and is a member of the IEEE, ACM, and ARRL.

I'd like to thank Ritika Singh for shepherding this book through the publishing process at Packt Publishing as well as for her suggestions throughout the process. I'd also like to thank the technical reviewers who provided their time to give suggestions and clarifications for each draft of the book. Of course, in the end, I'm responsible for any errors that might remain!

About the Reviewers

Lee Zhi Eng is a 3D artist-turned-programmer who worked as a game artist and game programmer in several local game studios in his country before becoming a contractor and a part-time lecturer at a local university, teaching game development subjects, particularly related to Unity Engine and Unreal Engine 4. You can find more information about him at http://www.zhieng.com.

Andrea Flesca is an Italian electronic engineer working in the software world for Selex ES, a primary Italian electronic systems and software provider, which has now become the IT division of Finmeccanica.

He has more than 15 years of software development experience, supporting the complete software life cycle management: requirement analysis and management, system architecture and design, C++/Java implementation, documentation and tests and validation. Also, his work focuses on technical solutions, design patterns, middleware, team leadership and mentoring, and customer relationships.

He has gained experience in GIS solutions through open source and ESRI technology, GIS analysis and development, web applications, cross-platform development, distributed computing systems, JEE and SOA architectures, enterprise service bus, and enterprise architecture integration.

He has worked for bank systems, telecommunications, and defense and currently works for smart cities and systems as an integration engineer.

From 2014, Andrea has been collaborating with Packt Publishing as a technical reviewer.

He loves rock music and prepares a great tiramisu. He can be contacted on LinkedIn.

To my beloved wife, Sara, and my lovely son, Gabriele.

Niels Holst graduated from the University of Copenhagen, Denmark, with a PhD in Biology and a BSc in Computer Science. He currently works at Aarhus University, Denmark, where he applies computer science to solve problems in Applied Ecology. He is a leader of the Universal Simulator open source project.

Sudhendu Kumar has been a GNU/Linux user for more than 6 years. Presently, he is a software developer for a networking giant. In his free time, he contributes to KDE.

I would like to thank the publisher for giving me this opportunity to review the book. I hope that you find the book useful as well as enjoy reading it and playing around with Qt/QML applications.

www.PacktPub.com

Support files, eBooks, discount offers, and more

For support files and downloads related to your book, please visit www.PacktPub.com.

Did you know that Packt offers eBook versions of every book published, with PDF and ePub files available? You can upgrade to the eBook version at www.PacktPub.com and as a print book customer, you are entitled to a discount on the eBook copy. Get in touch with us at service@packtpub.com for more details.

At www.PacktPub.com, you can also read a collection of free technical articles, sign up for a range of free newsletters and receive exclusive discounts and offers on Packt books and eBooks.

https://www2.packtpub.com/books/subscription/packtlib

Do you need instant solutions to your IT questions? PacktLib is Packt's online digital book library. Here, you can search, access, and read Packt's entire library of books.

Why subscribe?

- Fully searchable across every book published by Packt
- Copy and paste, print, and bookmark content
- On demand and accessible via a web browser

Free access for Packt account holders

If you have an account with Packt at www.PacktPub.com, you can use this to access PacktLib today and view 9 entirely free books. Simply use your login credentials for immediate access.

Table of Contents

Preface   **1**

Chapter 1: Getting Started with Qt Creator   **7**

Downloading Qt and Qt Creator   **8**

Finding your way around Qt Creator   **10**

Your first application – Hello World   **11**

Hello World using the QtGui library   **13**

Hello World using Qt Quick   **17**

Summary   **21**

Chapter 2: Building Applications with Qt Creator   **23**

Getting started – our sample library   **23**

Learning the landscape – the Build menu and the .pro files   **27**

Linking against our sample library   **30**

Getting lost and found again – debugging   **35**

Setting breakpoints and stepping through your program   37

Examining variables and memory   39

Examining the call stack   41

The Projects pane and building your project   **42**

A review – running and debugging your application   **44**

Summary   **45**

Chapter 3: Designing Your Application with Qt Designer   **47**

Code interlude – signals and slots   **48**

Creating forms in Qt Designer   **52**

Creating the main form   52

Using application resources   57

Instantiating forms, message boxes, and dialogs in your application   **58**

Wiring the Qt Widgets' application logic   **63**

Learning more about Qt Widgets   66

Code interlude – Qt Quick and the QML syntax   **67**

Creating Qt Quick applications in Qt Designer   **70**

    Creating a reusable button   71

    The calculator's main view   74

    Learning more about Qt Quick and QML   77

Summary   **77**

Chapter 4: Qt Foundations   **79**

Representing data using Qt's core classes   **80**

    Working with key-value pairs   82

Multithreading in Qt   **84**

Accessing files using Qt   **86**

Accessing HTTP resources using Qt   **89**

    Performing HTTP requests   91

Parsing XML using Qt   **92**

    Using XML parsing with HTTP   93

    Implementing WorkerThread   95

Summary   **98**

Chapter 5: Developing Applications with Qt Widgets   **99**

Your main application and its menus   **100**

Simple Qt Widgets   **103**

Managing the widget layout with layouts   **107**

Model-view-controller programming with Qt   **109**

    Analyzing a concrete model subclass   111

Rendering web content with QWebView   **113**

Summary   **115**

Chapter 6: Drawing with Qt   **117**

What we need to start drawing with Qt   **118**

Drawing with QPainter on QPaintDevice instances   **118**

Drawing off screen   **122**

Creating custom widgets   **123**

The Graphics View Framework   **127**

Summary   **137**

Chapter 7: Doing More with Qt Quick   **139**

The fundamental concepts of Qt Quick   **139**

States and transitions in Qt Quick   **149**

Integrating Qt Quick and C++   **154**

Putting it all together – an image gallery application   **156**

Summary   **167**

Chapter 8: Multimedia and Qt Quick — 169

Multimedia in Qt — 169
Playing audio clips and sound effects — 170
Playing video clips — 173
Accessing the camera — 175
Summary — 177

Chapter 9: Sensors and Qt Quick — 179

Sensors in Qt — 179
Determining the device location — 182
Obtaining a device's position – a simple example — 186
Summary — 191

Chapter 10: Localizing Your Application with Qt Linguist — 193

Understanding the task of localization — 194
Marking strings for localization — 195
Localizing your application with QLinguist — 196
Including localized strings in your application — 198
Localizing special parameters – currencies and dates with QLocale — 199
Summary — 200

Chapter 11: Optimizing Performance with Qt Creator — 201

The QML performance analyzer — 202
QtSlowButton – a Qt Quick application in need of performance tuning — 202
Finding memory leaks with Valgrind — 206
QtLeakyButton – a Qt C++ application in need of memory help — 207
Summary — 210

Chapter 12: Developing Mobile Applications with Qt Creator — 211

A mobile software development primer — 212
User attention is at a premium — 212
Computational resources are at a premium — 213
Network resources are at a premium — 214
Storage resources are at a premium — 215
To port or not to port? — 215
A word on testing — 216
Setting up Qt Creator for Android — 217
Downloading all the pieces — 217
Setting environment variables — 218
Finishing the Android SDK installation — 219
Configuring Qt Creator — 220
Building and running your application — 223

Supporting other mobile platforms   **223**
Summary   **223**
Chapter 13: Qt Tips and Tricks   **225**
Writing console applications with Qt Creator   **225**
Integrating Qt Creator with version control systems   **227**
Configuring the coding style and coding format options   **230**
Building projects from the command line   **232**
Setting the Qt Quick window display options   **233**
Learning more about Qt   **235**
Debugging Qt's signal-slot connections   **237**
Summary   **238**
Index   **239**

Preface

Whether you're just getting started with programming or you've settled on Qt as the GUI toolkit for your project, Qt Creator is a great choice for an Integrated Development Environment (IDE). In this book, we work to help you make the most of Qt and Qt Creator, showing you almost every facet of using Qt Creator, from its configuration through compiling and debugging applications along with numerous tips and tricks. Along the way, you gain valuable experience not just with Qt Creator as an IDE, but with Qt and Qt Quick as well. After reading this book, you'll be able to:

- Edit, compile, debug, and run C++ applications using Qt Creator, opening a path to build state-of-the-art console and GUI applications with Qt and with the Standard Template Library (STL)

- Edit, compile, debug, and run Qt Quick applications using Qt Creator, giving you access to one of the most advanced declarative GUI authoring environments anywhere

- Design GUI applications using Qt Designer to build either traditional widget-based or Qt Quick applications

- Analyze the memory and the runtime performance of your Qt applications, make improvements, and fix defects

- Provide localized versions of your application so that you can deploy it all over the world in different languages

- Use Qt Quick and Qt Widgets to write mobile applications for platforms such as Google Android

- Build multimedia- and sensor-aware applications with Qt's support for multimedia and sensors

What this book covers

This book is divided into thirteen chapters, which you should plan to read in order, especially if you're new to Qt Creator and Qt programming in general. These chapters are given as follows:

Chapter 1, Getting Started with Qt Creator, shows you how to download and install Qt Creator as well as edit simple applications to test your installation.

Chapter 2, Building Applications with Qt Creator, shows you how to compile, run, and debug your application using Qt Creator. You will learn how Qt Creator integrates with both the GNU debugger and the Microsoft console debugger to provide breakpoints, memory inspection, and other debugging help.

Chapter 3, Designing Your Application with Qt Designer, shows you how to use the drag-and-drop GUI designer that is a part of Qt Creator to build both Qt Widget-based applications and Qt Quick applications.

Chapter 4, Qt Foundations, takes you through the foundations of software development using Qt and also covers its support for platform-agnostic application development.

Chapter 5, Developing Applications with Qt Widgets, shows you how to build applications using Qt Widgets that look and act like native desktop applications on the platform of your choice.

Chapter 6, Drawing with Qt, shows the various ways you can move beyond the built-in controls in Qt and make your own drawing on the screen and other drawable entities such as image files in PNG or JPEG.

Chapter 7, Doing More with Qt Quick, expands on what you learned about Qt Quick in the introductory chapters.

Chapter 8, Multimedia and Qt Quick, introduces you to Qt Quick's support for multimedia, such as audio and video playback as well as how to use a camera if it is connected.

Chapter 9, Sensors and Qt Quick, shows you how to use the various sensors on many of the devices available today using Qt Quick.

Chapter 10, Localizing Your Application with Qt Linguist, shows you how to manage resource strings for different locales, letting you build your application with different languages in different locales.

Chapter 11, Optimizing Performance with Qt Creator, shows you how to use Qt Creator to examine your Qt Quick application's runtime performance, as well as how to perform the memory profiling of your application with Valgrind, an open source diagnostic tool.

Chapter 12, Developing Mobile Applications with Qt Creator, gives you a glimpse of the exciting arena of mobile software development and shows you how you can use what you've learned in this book about Qt and Qt Creator to write applications for platforms such as Google Android.

Chapter 13, Qt Tips and Tricks, is packed with tricks for using Qt and Qt Creator that will help you use the Qt framework and the Qt Creator IDE efficiently.

What you need for this book

Qt and Qt Creator are cross-platform tools. Whether you're using a Windows machine, a Macintosh using Mac OS X, or a workstation running Linux, you probably have what you need. You should have a reasonable amount of disk space (around 10 GB is enough) to install the whole Qt Creator IDE and Qt libraries. As with any software development environment, the more RAM you have, the better (although I've run Qt Creator on netbooks running Ubuntu with a gigabyte of RAM and survived!).

You should have a basic understanding of computer programming and be prepared to write code in C++. Knowledge of JavaScript is helpful if you're interested in programming with Qt Quick, but you can pick that up along the way with little difficulty.

Who this book is for

If you have little or no experience with Qt and Qt Creator, and might be using it for the first time as part of a college class or an open source project, or you just want to experiment with the platform and the IDE, this is the book for you.

I would especially encourage you to read this book if you're a student using Qt Creator in your university class on C++ programming! You should focus on the first two chapters and as much of the rest as you need for your course.

Conventions

In this book, you will find a number of text styles that distinguish between different kinds of information. Here are some examples of these styles and an explanation of their meaning.

Code words in text, database table names, folder names, filenames, file extensions, pathnames, dummy URLs, user input, and Twitter handles are shown as follows: "Finally, we have to add the `on_exitButton_clicked` method declaration to `mainwindow.h` if it's not already added."

A block of code is set as follows:

```
QApplication a(argc, argv);
QTranslator translator;
bool result = translator.load("QtLinguistExample-epo.qm");
a.installTranslator(&translator);
return a.exec();
```

When we wish to draw your attention to a particular part of a code block, the relevant lines or items are set in bold:

```
QApplication a(argc, argv);
QTranslator translator;
bool result = translator.load("QtLinguistExample-epo.qm");
a.installTranslator(&translator);
return a.exec();
```

Any command-line input or output is written as follows:

```
# % lupdate -pro .\QtLinguistExample.pro -ts .\QtLinguistExample-epo.ts
```

New terms and **important words** are shown in bold. Words that you see on the screen, for example, in menus or dialog boxes, appear in the text like this: "In Qt Creator, select **New File or Project...** from the **File** menu."

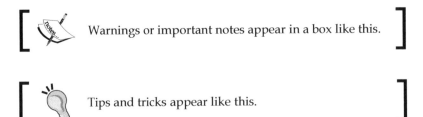

Warnings or important notes appear in a box like this.

Tips and tricks appear like this.

Reader feedback

Feedback from our readers is always welcome. Let us know what you think about this book—what you liked or disliked. Reader feedback is important for us as it helps us develop titles that you will really get the most out of.

To send us general feedback, simply e-mail feedback@packtpub.com, and mention the book's title in the subject of your message.

If there is a topic that you have expertise in and you are interested in either writing or contributing to a book, see our author guide at www.packtpub.com/authors.

Customer support

Now that you are the proud owner of a Packt book, we have a number of things to help you to get the most from your purchase.

Downloading the example code

You can download the example code files from your account at http://www.packtpub.com for all the Packt Publishing books you have purchased. If you purchased this book elsewhere, you can visit http://www.packtpub.com/support and register to have the files e-mailed directly to you.

Errata

Although we have taken every care to ensure the accuracy of our content, mistakes do happen. If you find a mistake in one of our books—maybe a mistake in the text or the code—we would be grateful if you could report this to us. By doing so, you can save other readers from frustration and help us improve subsequent versions of this book. If you find any errata, please report them by visiting http://www.packtpub.com/submit-errata, selecting your book, clicking on the **Errata Submission Form** link, and entering the details of your errata. Once your errata are verified, your submission will be accepted and the errata will be uploaded to our website or added to any list of existing errata under the Errata section of that title.

To view the previously submitted errata, go to https://www.packtpub.com/books/content/support and enter the name of the book in the search field. The required information will appear under the **Errata** section.

Piracy

Piracy of copyrighted material on the Internet is an ongoing problem across all media. At Packt, we take the protection of our copyright and licenses very seriously. If you come across any illegal copies of our works in any form on the Internet, please provide us with the location address or website name immediately so that we can pursue a remedy.

Please contact us at copyright@packtpub.com with a link to the suspected pirated material.

We appreciate your help in protecting our authors and our ability to bring you valuable content.

Questions

If you have a problem with any aspect of this book, you can contact us at questions@packtpub.com, and we will do our best to address the problem.

1
Getting Started with Qt Creator

Qt Creator is an integrated software development environment that supports both traditional C++ application development as well as development using the Qt project's libraries (collectively called **Qt** and pronounced as **cute**).

Qt is available under a commercial license as well as under GPL v3 and LGPL v2. Its development dates all the way back to 1991. For the first ten years of its life, it was a cross-platform toolkit for Windows and X11; by 2001, support for Mac OS X was added.

In this chapter, we will take a look at everything you need to get started:

- Where to download Qt Creator for Linux, Mac OS X, and Windows
- How to ensure that your basic configuration is running
- A quick look at a simple QtGui application as well as a Qt Quick application

Downloading Qt and Qt Creator

Qt, the cross-platform toolkit behind Qt Creator, has had a long and illustrious history. Presently a project of Digia, it has its own URL at `http://qt-project. org/` and has both commercial and non-commercial licenses. To get started with the non-commercial version for free, go to `http://qt-project.org/downloads` to see something similar to what the following screenshot shows:

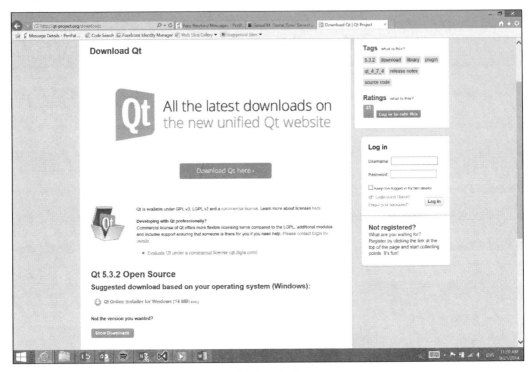

Downloading Qt Creator

One of the most popular platforms for application development with Qt is Linux. On many Linux variants—notably Ubuntu, my personal favorite—you can get Qt Creator using the package manager. On my Ubuntu box, Qt Creator is just a `sudo apt-get install qtcreator` command away. You'll get a version of Qt that matches your flavor of Linux, although it might not be the latest and greatest build from Digia.

By following the link and downloading Qt, you should now have Qt, Qt Creator, and the MinGW toolkit for developing software on Windows. If you're developing on Linux or Mac, the process will be similar, although it won't include MinGW.

Some downloads include the C++ compiler and the linker that you need for your development, while others don't. For example, on Windows, there's a variant that includes the MinGW tool chain, so you have everything you need to build applications. However, you can also download Qt Creator for Windows that uses the Microsoft Visual Studio compilers. So, if you prefer using Visual Studio for your compilation and Qt Creator as your IDE, this is also an option. On Mac OS X, you'll need to have Xcode and the command-line development tools installed first; you can download Xcode from the Mac OS X App Store and then use Xcode to download the command-line development tools.

Once the installer downloads, run it in the usual way. It'll launch an installation wizard for your platform, and installation should typically take about 3 to 4 minutes. You'll want to have plenty of disk space. Qt Creator doesn't consume that much disk space, but software development does; figure at least 500 MB for the tools and libraries, and budget a few gigabytes free on your main drive for your source code, intermediate object files, debugging symbols, and of course, your compiled application. (It is especially important to plan for this if you're running Qt Creator on a virtual machine; make sure that the virtual hard drive for your virtual machine image has plenty of disk space.)

You should also ensure that your development box has plenty of RAM; the more the better. Qt Creator runs happily on 2 GB of RAM, but the compiler and linker used by Qt Creator can run a lot faster if they have more RAM available.

Finding your way around Qt Creator

The following screenshot shows what you will see when you launch Qt Creator for the first time. Let's take a closer look at each portion of the screen, shown as follows:

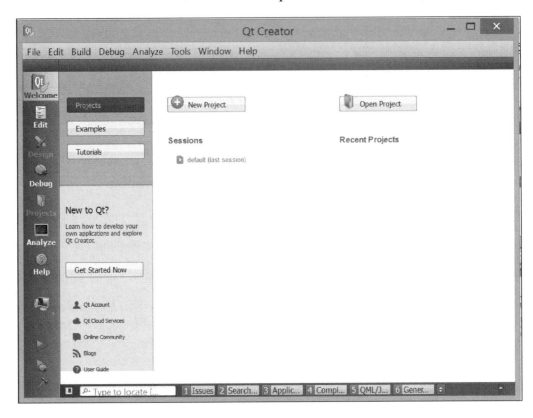

The main window, which currently shows the buttons for **New Project** and **Open Project**, is your *workspace*. The workspace also includes links to the Qt projects, examples, and tutorials as well as Qt's developer documentation, such as its online community and blogs. Under normal conditions, this will be located where you'll see the source code for your application. Along the left-hand side of the screen are a series of icons that let you select various views in your application. They are as follows:

- The **Welcome** mode, which shows basic information about Qt Creator
- The **Edit** mode, which lets you edit the files that make up your application
- The **Design** mode, which lets you use Qt Designer to design the user interface for your application

- The **Debug** mode, which lets you debug your application while it's running, including doing things such as viewing the memory and variables, setting breakpoints, and stepping through the application

- The **Projects** mode, which lets you adjust the build and link settings for your project

- The **Analyze** mode, which lets you profile your application's runtime performance

- The **Help** mode, which provides documentation on Qt Creator and the Qt framework

Let's create a new project using C++.

Your first application – Hello World

In Qt Creator, select **New File or Project...** from the **File** menu. Qt Creator will present you with the **New Project** wizard, which lets you choose the kind of project you want to create, give it a name, and so forth. To create your first application, perform the following steps:

1. Select **New File or Project...** if you haven't done so already.

2. Qt Creator presents you with a dialog that has a dizzying array of project choices. Choose **Application**, then **Qt Console Application**, and then click on **Choose....**

3. Qt Creator asks you for a name and a path to the directory where you want to store the files for the project. For the name, enter `HelloWorldConsole` and choose a path that makes sense to you (or accept the default). Then, click on **Next**.

4. Qt Creator can support various kits and libraries against which you can build an application. Select the Desktop Qt Kit, which should have been installed by default, leaving both the **Release** and **Debug** choices checked. Then, click on **Next**.

5. In the next step, Qt Creator prompts you about the version control for your project. Qt Creator can use your installed version control clients to perform change tracking for your project. For now, skip this and leave **Add to version control** set to **None**. Then, click on **Finish**.

Qt Creator creates your project and switches to the **Edit** view. In the source code editor for the `main.cpp` file, enter the following code:

```
#include <QCoreApplication>
#include <iostream>

using namespace std;

int main(int argc, char *argv[])
{
QCoreApplication a(argc, argv);

    cout << "Hello world!";

  return a.exec();
}
```

Downloading the example code

You can download the example code files for all Packt books you have purchased from your account at `http://www.packtpub.com`. If you purchased this book elsewhere, you can visit `http://www.packtpub.com/support` and register to have the files e-mailed directly to you.

The `QCoreApplication` task handles the entire system startup for an application, and every Qt Console app needs to create one and call its `exec` method as part of your `main` method. It sets up Qt's event handler and provides a bunch of porting helpers to determine things such as your application directory, library paths, and other details.

For a console application, that's all you need; you can freely mix and match Qt classes with the C++ standard library and Standard Template Library (although once you master Qt's foundation classes, many STL constructs might feel somewhat limiting).

Next, let's compile and run the application. There are several ways to do this. You can:

- Click on the green Run arrow below the **Help** view button on the left to run the application
- Hit *F5* to build and run your application in the debugger
- Click on **Start Debugging**… from the **Debug** menu

- Click on the green Run arrow with the bug over the arrow in order to debug the application on the left

- Choose **Run** from the **Build** menu (or hit *Ctrl + R*)

 If you only want to build the application, you can click on the hammer icon below the Run and Debug icons.

When you choose one of these options, Qt Creator invokes the compiler and the linker to build your application. If you choose the **Debug** option, Qt Creator switches to the **Debug** view (which we will discuss in detail in the next chapter) as it starts your application.

Once the application starts, you'll see the **Hello world!** message in a console view.

Hello World using the QtGui library

One of Qt's strengths is its rich collection of GUI elements that you can use to create windowed applications. Making a GUI application is similar in principle to making a console application; instead of choosing **Qt Console Application**, select **Qt Widgets Application** from the **New** dialog presented when you choose **New File or Project**. Try it now:

1. First, close the current file and project by clicking on **Close All Projects and Editors** from the **File** menu.

2. Next, click on **New File or Project**... again and click on **Qt Widgets Application** from the first step of the wizard.

3. Walk through the wizard again, naming your project `HelloWorldGui`.

4. Then, select the default kit. The **New** project wizard will prompt you for the name of the class implementing your main window. Leave the subclass as `QMainWindow` and the name as `MainWindow`. Skip the version control dialog portion of the wizard.

Qt Creator creates a default subclass of the class that provides the platform's basic window in the `mainform.h` and `mainform.cpp` files, and creates a form that will contain the widgets for your application's window.

The following screenshot shows a default form as you're editing it in Qt Designer. If you run the application at this point, you'll see an empty window. Instead, double-click on the `Forms` folder in the project tree (the second pane) of Qt Creator and then double-click on the `mainwindow.ui` file. Qt Creator switches to the `Design` view, and you'll see something similar to the next screenshot:

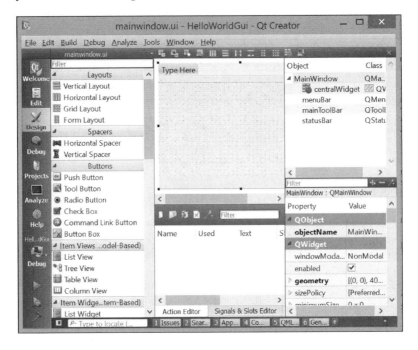

On the left-hand side is a list of the *layouts* that you can choose to organize widgets, such as spacers, views, containers, buttons, and other widgets; on top of this, there are various edit and layout options. In the middle is a view of the layout of your application's main window, and to the right are panes with a hierarchy of objects in your main window and the properties of any item that you click on in the main window.

While we will explore Qt Designer more in *Chapter 3, Designing Your Application with Qt Designer*, you can get a feel of using it to build a simple UI. Begin by ensuring that you're in the **Designer** mode:

1. Where it says **Type Here**, right-click and choose **Remove menu bar**.

2. Drag a label (under **Display Widgets** in the left-hand side pane) and drop it in the window preview in the center pane.

3. Double-click on the label that appears and type `Hello world!`.

4. Grab a corner of the label and resize it so that the entire text is shown. You can also move it around in the window.

5. Note that when you click on the label, the **Property** field in the lower-right pane is updated to show the properties of your new label.

6. Drag a button (under **Buttons** in the left-hand side pane) and drop it in the window preview in the center pane.

7. Double-click on the button and change its text to Exit.

8. With the new button selected, change the **objectName** field in the **Property** browser to exitButton.

9. Right-click on the button and select **Go to slot....** A window appears with a list of slots (for now, you can think of a slot as something that is triggered on an action; we will discuss them more in *Chapter 2, Building Applications with Qt Creator*).

10. Choose **clicked()** from the list that appears.

11. Qt Creator returns to the **Edit** view for your mainwindow.cpp file. Change it to read as follows:

```cpp
#include "mainwindow.h"
#include "ui_mainwindow.h"
#include <QApplication>
MainWindow::MainWindow(QWidget *parent) :
    QMainWindow(parent),
    ui(new Ui::MainWindow)
{
    ui->setupUi(this);
}

MainWindow::~MainWindow()
{
    delete ui;
}

voidMainWindow::on_exitButton_clicked()
{
    QApplication::exit();
}
```

Before running your application, let's be sure that you understand the implementation of the MainWindow class. The constructor of the MainWindow class loads the description of the user interface for the main window and sets it up using the Qt Creator-generated class Ui::MainWindow. The destructor deletes the implementation of the code layout, and the on_exitButton_clicked method simply terminates the application by calling the exit static method implemented by the QApplication class.

Finally, we have to add the `on_exitButton_clicked` method declaration to `mainwindow.h` if it's not already added. Double-click on this file in the browser on the left and make sure that it reads as follows:

```
#ifndef MAINWINDOW_H
#define MAINWINDOW_H

#include <QMainWindow>

namespaceUi {
class MainWindow;
}

class MainWindow : public QMainWindow
{
    Q_OBJECT

public:
    explicit MainWindow(QWidget *parent = 0);
    ~MainWindow();

private slots:
    void on_exitButton_clicked();

private:
    Ui::MainWindow *ui;
};

#endif // MAINWINDOW_H
```

The key lines you need to add are highlighted in the previous listing.

We'll learn more about signals and slots in the next chapter; for now, it's enough for you to know that you're declaring a private function to be triggered when you click on the button.

Run the application. It should open a single window with the text **Hello World!**; clicking on the **Exit** button in the window (or on the close box in the upper-right corner) should close the application. At this point, if you think you want to learn more about Qt Widget applications, go ahead and try dragging other GUI items to the window, or explore the help documentation for Qt Widget applications by switching to the **Help** view and clicking on **Qt GUI** from the list of help items.

Hello World using Qt Quick

Qt Quick is Qt's newer declarative framework for the user interface, and with this, it's incredibly easy to create fluid applications with animated transitions and flowing user interfaces. Using Qt Quick, you can describe your user interface using QML, a JavaScript-like language that lets you declare user interface elements and how they relate; the Qt Quick runtime does most of the heavy lifting in the implementation of your application.

By now, you can guess how to create a Qt Quick project. Choose **New File or Project** from the **File** menu, click on **Qt Quick Application,** and then follow the wizard.

The wizard will ask you one additional question: the Qt Quick version to use. You should simply choose the latest version. Once you walk through the wizard, you end up with a simple application that actually displays **Hello World** in its own window. Here's the code that it supplies:

```
import QtQuick 2.3

Rectangle {
    visible: true
    width: 360
    height: 360

    MouseArea {
        anchors.fill: parent
        onClicked: {
            Qt.quit();
        }
    }

    Text {
        text: qsTr("Hello World")
        anchors.centerIn: parent
    }
}
```

If you know JavaScript, the syntax of this might look a little familiar, but it's still different. The first two lines are the `import` statements; they indicate which classes should be available to the QML runtime. At a minimum, all of your Qt Quick applications must import `QtQuick`, as this one does.

The QML follows. It declares a parent rectangle of 360 × 360 pixels that determines the size of the application window. Inside the rectangle are two objects: a `Text` object and `MouseArea`. The `Text` object is just that: a label with the text `Hello World` placed in the center of the rectangle. Note that the value of the text property is actually the result of a function call to the `qsTr` function, which is Qt's built-in localization function. This looks at application resources to return the localized version of `Hello World` if it has been provided.

`MouseArea` is an object that takes user input and can execute functions based on this input; it's sized to fit the parent (`anchors.fill` is set to `parent`) and responds when clicked by executing the function assigned to the `onClicked` property. This `onClicked` function just exits the application by calling the Qt class's `quit` function.

At this point, you can run the application in the usual way, and you'll see a window with the text **Hello World** in the center of the window.

While the principles are similar, the Qt Quick designer is very different from the Qt Widgets designer. Take a look at the next screenshot:

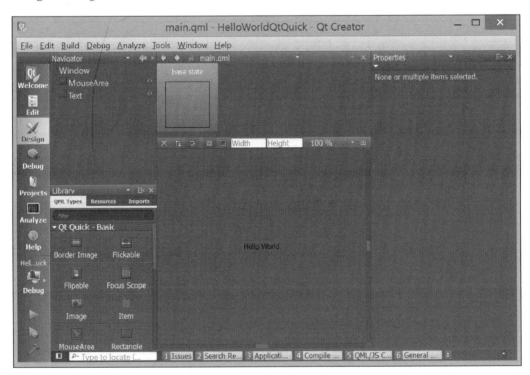

There are some obvious similarities: both designers show a list of things that you can add to a view, along with a hierarchy of the objects in the view and the properties of individual objects.

However, there are far fewer Qt Quick widgets than there are Qt widgets, and the widgets in Qt Quick don't match the look and feel of the native platform to nearly the same extent. That's by design; Qt Widgets is for building conventional applications that match the native platform by using native controls and a native look and feel, while Qt Quick is used for creating device-independent applications with their own look and feel. For example, you'd probably write an enterprise data collection application using Qt Widgets, while you'd create a media center application using Qt Quick.

However, the manner of using the designer is the same in both cases. Let's add another `MouseArea` to the main view and give it something to do:

1. Select `main.qml` from the list of files in Qt Creator and click on **Design** to see the **Design** view.

2. In the **Library** pane, select **QML Types** and scroll down until you see **Rectangle**. Drag the rectangle to the center pane and drop it somewhere above the **Hello World** label. You might need to resize the rectangle so that the label is still visible.

3. With the rectangle selected in the window pane, enter a color for your rectangle under **Colors**.

4. Now, drag a **MouseArea** object out of the **Library** pane and drop it on your new rectangle.

5. With the **MouseArea** object selected, click on **Layout** in the **Properties** tab and mouse over the layouts until you see **Fill to Parent**. (This is the fifth icon below **Anchors** and looks like a box with a border.) Click on it.

6. Go back to the **Edit** view and modify `main.qml` to look similar to the following code snippet:

```
Import QtQuick 2.3
import QtQuick.Window 2.2

Window {
    visible: true
    width: 360
    height: 360

    MouseArea {
        anchors.fill: parent
        onClicked: {
            Qt.quit();
```

```
            }
        }

        Text {
            id: text
            text: qsTr("Hello World")
            anchors.centerIn: parent
        }

        Rectangle {
            id: rectangle1
            x: 135
            y: 50
            width: 100
            height: 100
            color: "#708fff"

            MouseArea {
                id: mouseArea1
                anchors.fill: parent
                onClicked: text.text = qsTr("Hi there!")
            }
        }
    }
```

You can see that most of the changes were made by the **Design** view; it added a rectangle inside the original **MouseArea** object and another **MouseArea** object inside it. You will need to add a line giving the text element an ID of the text and the onClicked handler to the new **MouseArea** object that you dragged out in the **Design** view. The id property lets other QML access the text field by name (in this case, its name is simply text), and the onClicked handler changes the contents of the text item's text property to the text **Hi there!**.

It's worth making a note of qsTr here; you don't have to add any text to the application resources to get basic localization working. This is unlike most other platforms where localization occurs by providing keys to values in local files for strings with a default value for the unlocalized strings.

Run the application. You'll see your rectangle above the text **Hello World**, and clicking on the rectangle changes the text to read **Hi there!**.

Summary

Getting Qt Creator is easy; it's just a web download away, or on most Linux platforms, it's an optional installation through the native package manager (although the versions delivered by a package manager might be slightly older than those you get from the Qt Project's website).

Qt Creator organizes its source code for you in projects; when you first launch it, you can either create a default project or create a new project to contain the source code and resources for your application. Inside Qt Creator are all the options you need to compile and debug your application. In addition, it supports designer tools for developing both Qt Widgets and Qt Quick applications.

In the next chapter, we'll dig into the details of how to configure Qt Creator for compiling and editing your code, including how to add source files to your project, configure compiler and linker options, add dependencies to third-party libraries, and so on.

2
Building Applications with Qt Creator

The first thing you would want to do with Qt Creator is figure out how to add source files and build (or debug) your project. This chapter is all about that—we'll go over how to add files to a project, how to create libraries in a project, and how to use the debugger and the console logger. At the end of this chapter, you'll be driving Qt Creator to develop console applications like a pro.

In this chapter, we will do the following:

- Learn about our sample library
- Look into the Build menu and the `.pro` files
- Link against our sample library
- Debug
- Build your project
- Run and debug your application

Getting started – our sample library

This chapter's example code has two pieces: a library that defines a public function and a console application that calls this function. Libraries are a great way to break up your applications, and while this example is simple, it also lets me show you how to create a library and include it in your application.

I'm going to stretch your imagination a bit; let's pretend that you're responsible for setting up a library of math functions. In this example, we'll only write one function, factorial. You should be able to recollect the factorial function from introductory programming; it's represented by a ! and is defined as follows:

- 0! is 0

- 1! is 1

- n! is n × (n - 1)!

This is a recursive definition and we can code it in the following way:

```
unsigned long factorial(unsigned int n)
{
    switch(n)
    {
        case 0: return 0;
        case 1: return 1;
        default: return n * factorial(n-1);
    }
}
```

An alternate definition that avoids the cost of function calls is given as follows:

```
unsigned long factorial(unsigned int n)
{
    unsigned long result = 1;
    for(unsigned int i = n; i > 1; i--)
    {
        result *= i;
    }
    return result;
}
```

Why did I pick the recursive definition? There are three reasons for this: I think that it's clearer, the function call's performance overhead isn't a big deal in this example, and many of you might be using this book as part of introductory Computer Science courses where recursion is taught and should be reinforced.

Let's begin by creating the library that implements our factorial function. To do this, follow these steps:

1. In Qt Creator, from the **File** menu, choose **New File or Project...**.

2. Select **Libraries** in the left-hand side pane of the dialog and select **C++ Library** from the center pane.

3. Qt Creator can create dynamic libraries (DLLs in Windows parlance), static libraries, or plugins that can be shared between applications. We're going to create a static library; so, in the next window that appears, select **Statically Linked Library** and name it `MathFunctions`. Choose a reasonable path for the project.

> A statically linked library is included in your program binary and is part of your application. If multiple applications use a static library, each will have its own copy. A dynamically linked library is stored as a separate file and can be shared by multiple applications at runtime because each application loads the dynamically linked library. Qt also supports plugins, which are dynamic libraries loaded at runtime that can extend an application's functionality.

4. In the next step of the wizard, leave the Qt version, Debug, and Release items checked.

5. Libraries built by Qt Creator can rely on the Qt libraries. Let this library rely on QtCore, the core data structures for Qt; in the **Select Required Modules** window, leave **QtCore** checked and click on **Next**.

6. In the next window, name the skeleton files that Qt Creator will add to your project. Click on **Next**.

7. In the **Project Management** window, choose **<None>** for the version control choice (we won't use version control for this project) and click on **Finish**.

8. Edit `mathfunctions.h` to include a static method declaration for our factorial function:

```
#ifndef MATHFUNCTIONS_H
#define MATHFUNCTIONS_H

class MathFunctions
{
```

```
public:
    MathFunctions();

    static unsigned long int factorial(unsigned int n);
};

#endif // MATHFUNCTIONS_H
```

9. Open `mathfunctions.cpp`. You can do this in one of the two or three ways available: either by double-clicking on it in the **Project** pane, by right-clicking on the factorial function and selecting **Switch Header/Source**, or by simply hitting the *F4* key. Write your factorial function; `mathfunctions.cpp` should now comprise something similar to this:

```
#include "mathfunctions.h"

MathFunctions::MathFunctions()
{
}

unsigned long int
MathFunctions::factorial(unsigned int n)
{
    switch(n)
    {
        case 0: return 0;
        case 1: return 1;
        default: return n * factorial(n-1);
    }
}
```

10. Click on the **Projects** button on the left-hand side and change the output paths for the **Release** and **Debug** builds to point to the same directory by editing the **Build directory** line under **General**, first for the **Build** and then for the **Debug** build configurations. To do this, remove the release and debug portions of the directory path from the **Build directory** path. This way, when you build your library, Qt Creator will place the release and debug builds of your library in folders named `release` and `debug`, respectively.

As you write the code, note that Qt Creator prompts you at various stages about things it can deduce from your header with automatic suggestions (called **autosuggest**). For example, once you type `MathFunc`, it offers to autocomplete the class name or the C preprocessor guard; you can select the class name either using the mouse or just hit *Return* to get the class name.

Similarly, typing the double colons tells Qt Creator that you're trying to enter something in the `MathFunctions` class, and it prompts you with the `MathFunctions` class members; you can use the arrows to select `factorial` and hit *Return*, and it will type that.

Finally, typing an opening parenthesis cues Qt Creator that you're defining a function, and it prompts you with the arguments to the function you defined in the header file. You'll see this autocompletion a lot when you type code; it's a great way to learn Qt too, because you can type a class name or part of a function name and Qt Creator prompts you with helpful hints along the way. Qt Creator can also autocomplete variable and method names; start typing a function name and press *Ctrl* + Space bar to see a menu of possible completions.

Before you continue, be sure to build your library in both the release and debug configurations. The easiest way to do this is to click on the build selector at the bottom-left of the software and select either **Release** or **Debug** and then click on the hammer icon to perform a build.

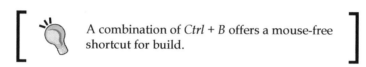

A combination of *Ctrl* + *B* offers a mouse-free shortcut for build.

Learning the landscape – the Build menu and the .pro files

In the previous chapter, you learned how to build applications by hitting the hammer button in the corner of Qt Creator's main window or by starting the debugger. To just build your library—or any application—you can either use the hammer icon or the various choices in the **Build** menu. The obvious choice is either **Build All** or **Rebuild All**; choosing **Build All** recompiles only those files that need to be rebuilt as recognized by Qt Creator; **Rebuild All** cleans the project of all the object files and rebuilds the entire project from scratch. In most cases, it's sufficient to choose **Build All**, and that's what you want to do because it's faster. Sometimes, you really do want to rebuild the whole project, when things are broken and Qt's Make system can't reconcile all the dependencies (or you've incorrectly specified them). Select **Build All** now and wait for it to build while we discuss the other options.

The **Build** menu lets you build a single file—it is handy if all you want to do is check the syntax of the code you're writing and to make sure that it is free of errors—or the entire project. It also lets you run the project outside the debugger, which you might want to do in some circumstances, such as when giving a demonstration. You can also clean your project (remove all object files and other autogenerated products) by selecting **Clean All**.

The **Publish** option is available for some add-on kits that let you publish compiled applications and libraries to application stores and repositories; you can find more details about this in the documentation for any Qt Creator add-in, such as the SDKs for Maemo development (an older Linux variant from Nokia for handheld devices).

Behind every Qt Creator project is a `.pro` file; this serves the same function as a Makefile, and in fact, it is processed by a Qt toolkit command called *qmake*.

 A Makefile is a file that describes how your application can be built using the utility make. For more information, go to `http://en.wikipedia.org/wiki/Make_(software)`. Qt provides qmake, a utility that converts the `.pro` files to Makefiles; you'll work with the Qt Creator GUI most of the time to create the `.pro` files and ignore the resulting Makefile.

These files are declarative; in that, you declare the relationships between the files that make up your application, and qmake figures out how to build your application from there. In most cases, you'll need to make a few or no changes to a `.pro` file, but it doesn't hurt to understand how they work. Double-click on `MathFunctions.pro` and you'll find this:

```
#-------------------------------------------------
#
# Project created by QtCreator 2013-07-23T19:50:46
#
#-------------------------------------------------

QT       -= gui

TARGET = MathFunctions
TEMPLATE = lib
CONFIG += staticlib

SOURCES += mathfunctions.cpp

HEADERS += mathfunctions.h
```

```
unix {
    target.path = /usr/lib
    INSTALLS += target
}
```

The basic syntax of a `.pro` file is variable assignments; the file generated by Qt Creator assigns the following variables:

- `QT`: This variable indicates the Qt modules that your project will link against. By default, all projects include QtCore and QtGui; there's a plethora of other modules available, which include key features such as the WebKit web browsing engine (QtWebkit) and multimedia libraries (Phonon). Our assignment here indicates that we use the default Qt modules but don't link them against QtGui.

- `TARGET`: This variable is the name of the compiled library or executable.

- `TEMPLATE`: This variable indicates the kind of template that qmake should use to generate the binary; in our case, we're saying that it should use the template to create a `lib` file—a static library.

- `CONFIG`: This variable passes an additional configuration to qmake's template; here, we say that we want a statically linked library.

- `SOURCES` and `HEADERS`: These variables contain lists of the source and header files that make up our project.

- `INSTALLS`: This variable indicates where the resulting build product should be installed. Here, it's set in a *scope*. Scopes let you specify conditional options in qmake; the condition for the scope is a variable or an expression, which might be true or false, and the code that follows is executed if the variable is true. The scope at the end of this file says, "if we're building for a Unix variant, set the `target.path` variable to `/usr/lib` and the `INSTALLS` variable to target."

These are the basic variables you'll find in almost any `.pro` file.

For a good discussion of qmake scopes that you can use to control conditional compilation, see `http://qt-project.org/doc/qt-4.8/qmake-advanced-usage.html`.

Two additional variables that you're likely to want to know about are DEFINES and LIBS; DEFINES lets you specify preprocessor defines that should be set throughout the build process, and LIBS indicates additional libraries against which Qt Creator should link your project.

Note how variables are managed: you use = for assignment, += to add an item to a list, and -= to remove an item from a list.

Linking against our sample library

Now, let's make an application that depends on our library. Our application will call the factorial function in the library, statically linking to the library in order to access the factorial function. To accomplish this, you need to perform the following steps:

1. Select **Close All Projects and Editors** from the **File** menu.

2. Choose **New File or Project...** from the **File** menu and create a new Qt console application called MathFunctionsTest using the wizard.

3. Right-click on **MathFunctionsTest** in the **Project** pane and click on **Add Library...**. You can now choose a library in your build tree, a library outside your build tree, an external library on your system such as the Unix math library, fftmpeg, or another library that you've created. Select **External Library** and click on **Next**.

4. Browse the library file that was built in the previous section by clicking on **Browse**, next to the line labelled **Library file**. It'll be in a folder named something such as build-MathFunctions-Desktop_Qt_5_3_0_ MinGW_32bit-Debug in your project's folder. Select the MathFunctions library in either the release or debug folders—it doesn't matter which. The dialog box should look something similar to the following screenshot:

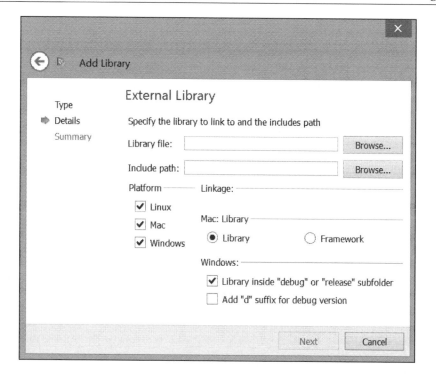

5. Browse the include files for your library by clicking on **Browse** next to **Include path**; this is the directory where you put the headers for your library.

6. Choose static linking.

7. Leave the other values set to their default values, click on **Next**, and then click on **Finish**.

Qt Creator will work its magic with your `.pro` file, adding a `LIBS` variable that includes the output of your library's build and an include path to your library's header files.

We can now call our factorial function. Edit `main.cpp` to read the following code:

```
#include <QCoreApplication>
#include "mathfunctions.h"

int main(int argc, char *argv[])
{
    QCoreApplication a(argc, argv);

    qDebug("6! is %lu", MathFunctions::factorial(6));
```

```
        return a.exec();
}
```

This code first includes our library header file. Note that if you compile the application after adding just the `#include` declaration, you'll get autosuggest help for every element of the `MathFunctions` library. This code uses `qDebug` instead of the C standard library to process its console output.

> `qDebug()` actually has a stream-savvy implementation too. I could have written the `qDebug` line as follows:
>
> ```
> qDebug() << "6! is" << MathFunctions::factorial(6);
> ```
>
> The code would have generated the same output. To do this, you'll need to be sure to include the line `#include <QDebug>`.

Build and run the application now in the **Debug** mode; you should see a console window with the text **6! is 720**. Now, try to build and run the library in the **Release** mode... wait, why is the debugging output from `qDebug` still there?

`qDebug` isn't really a debugging log; it's an output stream for debugging information regardless of build levels. If you want to turn off its output in release builds, you'll need to edit the `.pro` file. Double-click on your `.pro` file and add the following line:

```
CONFIG(release, debug|release): DEFINES += QT_NO_DEBUG_OUTPUT
```

This is another scope; it says that if your build configuration is `release`, add the `QT_NO_DEBUG_OUTPUT` preprocessor definition to the list of preprocessor definitions for the project.

Now, if you rebuild (you don't just choose build, but actually choose rebuild because you want a clean build through the entire system) and run in the release mode, you won't see any output.

> Qt actually defines four output streams, one for debugging messages and one for bonafide warnings. Use qDebug for regular logging and qWarning to output messages of a higher priority. There's also qCritical and qFatal for high-priority log messages that will indicate critical failures or failures that cause the application to terminate. You can also turn off warnings in release builds in the same way; simply add the following to your `.pro` file:
>
> ```
> CONFIG(release, debug|release): DEFINES +=
>     QT_NO_WARNING_OUTPUT
> ```

What will you do if you want to add files to your project? You can either do this by manually editing the .pro file—which can be faster if you're a good typist, but it is also error-prone and can result in weird build problems if you mess up—or by right-clicking on your project and selecting either **Add New...** or **Add Existing Files...**. The **Add New...** option opens up a short wizard with choices such as these:

- C++ header and source files

- Qt Designer forms, which we'll talk about in the next chapter

- Qt resource files, which we'll talk about in the next chapter

- **Qt Meta-object Language (QML) files**

- JavaScript files (which can contain the code implementing the logic of a Qt Quick application)

- OpenGL shaders for fragments or vertices in either full OpenGL or OpenGL/ES

- Text files (such as a `Readme` file for your project) or a scratch file to use as a place to stash temporary clipboard items until you're done with an editing session

Before we move on to the important topic of debugging, let's take a look at one more .pro file: the .pro file for our application:

```
#-------------------------------------------------
#
# Project created by QtCreator 2013-07-23T20:43:19
#
#-------------------------------------------------

QT       += core

QT       -= gui

CONFIG(release, debug|release):
DEFINES += QT_NO_DEBUG_OUTPUT

TARGET = MathFunctionsTest
CONFIG   += console
CONFIG   -= app_bundle

TEMPLATE = app

SOURCES += main.cpp
```

```
win32:CONFIG(release, debug|release): LIBS += -L$$PWD/../
    build-MathFunctions-Desktop_Qt_5_3_0_MinGW_32bit-Debug/release/
    -lMathFunctions
else:win32:CONFIG(debug, debug|release): LIBS += -L$$PWD/../
    build-MathFunctions-Desktop_Qt_5_3_0_MinGW_32bit-Debug/debug/
    -lMathFunctions
else:unix: LIBS += -L$$PWD/../
    build-MathFunctions-Desktop_Qt_5_3_0_MinGW_32bit-Debug/
    -lMathFunctions


INCLUDEPATH += $$PWD/../MathFunctions
DEPENDPATH += $$PWD/../MathFunctions


win32-g++:CONFIG(release, debug|release): PRE_TARGETDEPS +=
    $$PWD/../build-MathFunctions-Desktop_Qt_5_3_0_MinGW_32bit-Debug
    /release/libMathFunctions.a
else:win32-g++:CONFIG(debug, debug|release): PRE_TARGETDEPS +=
    $$PWD/../build-MathFunctions-Desktop_Qt_5_3_0_MinGW_32bit-Debug
    /debug/libMathFunctions.a
else:win32:!win32-g++:CONFIG(release, debug|release):
    PRE_TARGETDEPS += $$PWD/../
    build-MathFunctions-Desktop_Qt_5_3_0_MinGW_32bit-Debug
    /release/MathFunctions.lib
else:win32:!win32-g++:CONFIG(debug, debug|release):
    PRE_TARGETDEPS += $$PWD/../
    build-MathFunctions-Desktop_Qt_5_3_0_MinGW_32bit-Debug
    /debug/MathFunctions.lib
else:unix: PRE_TARGETDEPS += $$PWD/../
    build-MathFunctions-Desktop_Qt_5_3_0_MinGW_32bit-Debug
    /libMathFunctions.a
```

Phew! That's pretty dense. Let's see if we can unravel it. It begins by telling the build system that we use QtCore, but not QtGui. Next up is the instruction to disable the qDebug messages in release builds, which won't happen by default. The TARGET, CONFIG, and TEMPLATE options together say that we're building a console application with the name MathFunctionsTest. The next line indicates that we have one source file, main.cpp.

The next set of scopes indicate the path to our library and handle the fact that our libraries are in different directories on Windows for release and debug—this is different from Unix systems, where there is only one build variant of the library. After this come the INCLUDEPATH and DEPENDPATH variables, which indicate that there are library headers in the MathFunctions directory and that the application depends on those headers; so, if the timestamps on the headers change, the binary should be rebuilt.

The final scope specifies the same dependency on the output library itself; if the library changes, the application executables have to be rebuilt. This is especially important because that way, we can run multiple copies of Qt Creator, edit our library and application files separately, and rebuild the bits we need either after they change, as well as all the dependencies get figured out and the right bits get built automatically.

Getting lost and found again – debugging

Qt Creator has a state-of-the-art GUI that hooks into either the GNU debugger GDB, or Microsoft's command-line debugger CDB if you use Microsoft tools.

If you've installed Qt Creator on Mac OS or Linux or the MinGW version of Qt Creator for Windows, you have everything you need to begin debugging your application. If you already had Microsoft Visual Studio installed and then installed a version of Qt Creator that uses Microsoft's compiler, you also need to install the Microsoft command-line debugger to use Qt Creator's debugging features. Here's how you can install the command-line debugger:

1. Download the debugging tools for Windows, either from `http://msdn.microsoft.com/en-us/windows/hardware/hh852365` if you are using the 32-bit version of the compiler and Qt Creator, or from `http://msdn.microsoft.com/en-us/windows/hardware/hh852365` for the 64-bit version of the compiler and Qt Creator.

2. Configure the debugging symbol server by going to **Options** under the **Tools** menu, selecting the **Debugger** item on the left-hand side, clicking on the **CDB Paths** pane, and edit the textbox next to the **Symbol Paths** line.

Usually, the debugger works out of the box with Qt Creator, unless you're using the Microsoft tool chain. However, if you encounter problems, consult the Qt documentation about setting up the debugger at `http://qt-project.org/doc/qt-5/debug.html`.

The following screenshot shows the debugger in action with our test project, stopped at a breakpoint. Let's take a look at the following screenshot in detail to get oriented:

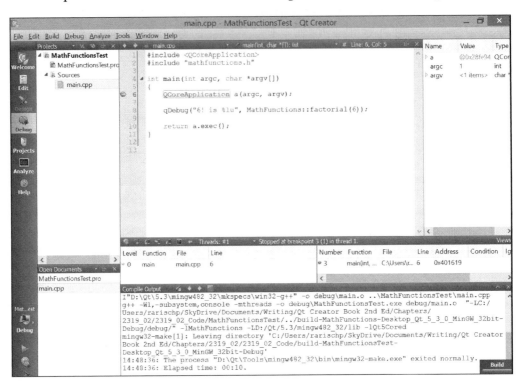

In the screenshot, you'll see the following components:

- On the left-hand side is the usual row of buttons to pick a view in Qt Creator
- Next to the buttons is the view of the project files and the list of open documents
- In the main editor pane, every source line has a clickable indicator to let you set and clear breakpoints
- The call stack, indicating how the program got to the line execution is stopped at, is shown in the pane below the editor pane
- In the upper-right corner is the variable inspector, where you can see the values of the variables in the current stack frame, along with any global variables
- Below the variable inspector is a list of pending breakpoints, so you can turn on and turn off breakpoints without needing to hunt through the code

To generate the screen that you can see in the preceding screenshot, I clicked to the left of line 6 placing a breakpoint and then clicked the **Debug** button on the left after ensuring I'd specified a **Debug** build in the build selector. Qt Creator built the application in the **Debug** mode, started the application, and let it run to the breakpoint on line 6.

Setting breakpoints and stepping through your program

A breakpoint, if you haven't encountered the idea before, is just that—a point at which execution breaks and you can examine the program's state. Once the execution is stopped at a breakpoint, you can step into a function or step over a line, executing your program one line at a time to see how it's behaving. Clicking to the left-hand side of a line number in the **Debug** view lets you set or clear breakpoints. While stopped at a breakpoint, a yellow-colored arrow in the margin of the editor pane indicates the line of code that the processor is about to execute.

While at a breakpoint, several buttons appear above the call stack pane that let you control the program flow, which you can see in the following screenshot:

The buttons are defined as follows:

- The green-colored Continue button, which continues execution at the line indicated by the arrow. You can also continue by pressing the *F5* function key.

- The red-colored Stop button, which stops debugging altogether.

- The Step Over button, which executes the current line and advances to the next line before stopping again. You can step over one line by pressing *F10*.

- The Step Into button, which enters the next function to be called and stops again. You can step into a function by pressing *F11*.

- The Step Out button, which runs the remainder of the function in the current calling context before stopping again. You can step out of the current function by pressing *Shift + F11*.

- The instruction-wise button (looks like a little screen), which toggles the debugger between working a source line at a time and an assembly line at a time.

- There's also a menu of threads, so you can see which thread is running or has stopped.

For example, (in the previous screenshot) from line 7 if we step over line 8 (pressing *F10*) and then press *F11*, we'll end up inside our factorial function. At this point, if we step into the function again, we'll see the value for *n* change in the right-hand side column, and the arrow advance to point toward line 9 (again, as numbered in the screenshot). From here, we can debug the factorial function in several ways:

- We can examine the contents of a variable by looking at it in the right-hand side pane. If it's in a stack frame above the current calling frame, we can change call frames and see variables in a different call frame too.

- We can modify a variable by clicking on its value and entering a new value.

- With some debuggers, we can move the arrow to different lines in the calling function to skip one or more lines of code or rewind the execution to rerun a segment of code again.

This last feature—which unfortunately doesn't work with the Microsoft Command-Line Debugger—is especially powerful, because we can step through a program, observe an error, modify variables to work around the course of the error, and continue testing the code without needing to recompile it and rerun the executable. Or, I can skip a bit of the code that I know takes a while to run by substituting the new state in the variables in question and continuing from a new location in the current call frame.

Also, there are a number of other things that we can do, from how we debug the application to various ways in which we can view the state of the application when it's running. From the main **Debug** menu, we can do the following:

- Detach the debugger from a running process by selecting **Detach** from the **Debug** menu (this is handy if the debugger is slowing things down and we know that part of our code doesn't need to be debugged).

- Interrupt the program execution by stopping the execution and examining the current state by choosing **Interrupt** from the **Debug** menu (useful if our application seems caught in a long loop we weren't expecting and appears hung).

- While it is stopped, run to the line that the cursor is on by choosing **Run to Line** or pressing *Ctrl + F10*.

- While it is stopped, skip to the line that the cursor is on by choosing **Jump to Line**. Choosing **Jump to Line** lets you skip the lines of code between the current point and the target line.

Examining variables and memory

The variables pane shows you the values of all the variables in the current stack frame. Structures show the values of their members, so you can walk through complex data structures as well. From the variables pane, you can also copy a variable name and value to the clipboard or just a variable value.

In the variables pane, there's a really useful feature called the **Expression Evaluator**, which lets you construct algebraic expressions for the variables in your code and see the results. For example, if I'm stopped at the beginning of the factorial function with n set to 6, I can right-click on the variables pane, choose **Insert New Expression Evaluator**, and type in a formula such as n* (n-1) in the dialog that appears. Thus, a new line appears in the pane showing the expression and the value 30. While this is a pretty contrived example, I can view pointer values and pointer dereferences as well.

I can also conditionally break the execution when a variable changes; this is called a conditional breakpoint or a data breakpoint. For example, let's put a loop in our main function and break as we execute the loop. To do this, first change main to read like the following block of code:

```
#include <QCoreApplication>
#include <QDebug>
#include "mathfunctions.h"

int main(int argc, char *argv[])
{
    QCoreApplication a(argc, argv);

    int values[] = { 6, 7, 8 };
    for(unsigned int i = 0; i < sizeof(values)/sizeof(int); i++)
    {
        qDebug() << values[i]
                << "! = "
                << MathFunctions::factorial(values[i]);
    }
    return a.exec();
}
```

This will walk the values stored in the integer array values and print the computed factorial of each value. Start debugging again, and let's add a data breakpoint on `i`. To do this, perform the following steps:

1. Put a breakpoint on the first line of `main`, the line initializing `QCoreApplication`.

2. Step over until the `for` loop, then right-click on `i` in the right pane, and choose **Add Data Breakpoint at Object's Address** from the **Add Data Breakpoint** submenu.

3. Continue by pressing *F5* or the **Continue** button.

The execution will stop at line 11, the beginning of the `for` loop, when `i` is set to `0`. Each time I hit *F5* to continue, the application runs until the value of `i` changes as a result of the `i++` statement at the end of the `for` loop.

You can also inspect and change the individual values of arrays in the variable inspector by clicking on the expansion arrow next to the array name in the variable inspector pane.

In addition to viewing and changing variable values, you can view and change individual memory locations. You might want to do this if you're debugging a decoder or encoder for a binary format, for example, where you need to see a specific location in the memory. From the variables pane, you have several choices by which you can check a memory location; a few of them are given as follows:

- You can right-click on a given variable and open a memory window at this variable's address

- You can right-click on a given variable and open a memory window at the value that the variable points to (in other words, dereference a pointer to a memory location)

- You can right-click on the variable pane and open up a memory browser at the beginning of the current stack frame

- You can right-click on the variable pane and open up a memory browser at an arbitrary location in the memory

The following screenshot shows the memory viewer showing the memory that contains the array values:

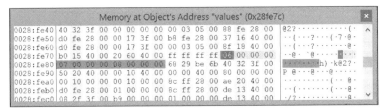

The window shows the memory addresses on the left-hand side, the values of the memory in 16 bytes to a line (first in hexadecimal and then in ASCII), and colors the actual variable you've selected to open the window. You can select a range of values and then right-click on them to do the following:

- Copy the values in ASCII or hexadecimal
- Set a data breakpoint on the memory location you've selected
- Transfer the execution to the address you've clicked (probably not what you want to do if you're viewing data!)

Examining the call stack

The *call stack* is the hierarchy of function calls in your application's execution at a point in time. Although the actual flow varies; typically in your code it begins in `main`, although what calls `main` differs from platform to platform. An obvious use for the call stack is to provide context when you click on the **Interrupt** button; if your program is just off contemplating its navel in a loop somewhere, clicking on **Interrupt** and taking a look at the call stack can give you a clue as to what's going on.

Remember how I defined the factorial function in terms of itself? You can see this very clearly if you put a breakpoint in the factorial and call it and then continue through the breakpoint a few times before looking at the call stack; you'll see something akin to the following screenshot:

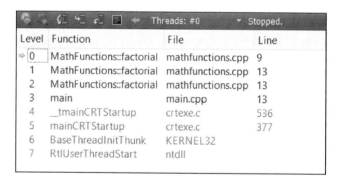

Working from left to right, the fields in the call stack window are the stack levels (numbering starts from the top of the stack and moves down), the functions being invoked, the files that the function is defined in, and the line numbers of the function currently being executed. So, this stack frame says that we're on line 9 of `MathFunctions::factorial` in `mathfunctions.cpp`, called by line 13 of `MathFunctions::factorial`, which is called by line 13 of `MathFunctions::factorial`... and so on, until it bottoms out in our `main` function and the system startup code that the operating system uses to set up the application process before that.

If you right-click on a line of the call stack pane, you can perform the following actions:

- Reload the stack, in case the display appears corrupted
- Copy the contents of the call stack to the clipboard—great for bug reports; if your application throws an exception or crashes in the debugger, you can copy the call stack and send it off to the developer responsible for that part of the code (or keep it for yourself as a souvenir)
- Open the memory editor at the address of the instruction at the line of code indicated by the function call in the call stack
- Open the disassembler at the address of the instruction at the line of code indicated by the function call in the call stack
- Disassemble a region of the memory or the current function
- Show the program's counter address in the call stack window while debugging

The Projects pane and building your project

You've seen how the `.pro` file affects your project's compilation, but there's even more to it than this. If you click on the **Projects** button on the left of Qt Creator, you'll see the project's options, which consist of the following:

- The **Build & Run** options
- The **Editor** options
- The **Code Style** options
- **Dependencies**

Each of these is in its own panel.

In most cases, you won't need to monkey around with any of these settings. But you might have to tinker with the **Build & Run** settings, especially if you're targeting multiple platforms such as Windows and Linux with cross-compilers or Android. (I will write more about this exciting development in Qt later in this book.)

The final thing that you should know is the build and run kit selector. Qt is one of the best cross-platform toolkits available today, and you can easily find yourself working on a system supporting multiple platforms, such as Linux and Android, or multiple versions of Qt. To support this, Qt has the notion of a build kit, which is just the headers, libraries, and associated things to support a specific platform. You can install multiple build kits and choose which build kit you're compiling against by choosing **Open Build and Run Kit Selector...**. By default, if you followed the steps in the previous chapter to install Qt Creator, you'll have one build kit installed; from the Digia site, you can choose others.

The different types of settings in the **Project** mode are as follows:

- For the build settings, there are configuration options for your release and debug builds. In the **Build** settings editor, you can control whether the build products are placed in their own directory (the default, a so-called shadow build where your build outputs are not mixed with the source code but placed in their own directory), the qmake configuration for the build (and actually see how Qt Creator will invoke qmake), how Qt Creator cleans your project, and any environment variables you need to set for the build.

- The run settings let you control whether your application runs locally or is deployed on a remote host (not always supported, but usually the case for platforms such as Android), any command-line arguments that you want to pass to your applications, and the settings for the performance analyzer tool, which I will talk about in *Chapter 4, Qt Foundations*.

- In the **Editor** panel, you can set specific editor options for this project. These override the global Qt Creator defaults, which you can set by choosing **Options** from the **Tools** menu and selecting the **Text Editor** option. These options include details such as whether to use tabs or spaces when formatting your code (I strongly suggest you use spaces; it's compatible with editors everywhere!), the number of spaces per tab stop, whether or not automatic indentation should occur, how source files should be encoded, and so forth.

- The **Code Style** panel is another override to the global settings for Qt Creator (this time, it's the C++ and Qt Quick panels of the **Options** dialog available from the **Options** menu). Here, you can pick the default styles or edit the styles.

 I'd strongly recommend that you pick a style that matches the existing source code you're editing; if you're starting from a blank page, the Qt default style is quite readable and is my favorite.

- The **Dependencies** panel lets you set the build order if your project file contains multiple subprojects so that things build in the right order. For example, we could choose to open both our library project and our test project; if we do, we'll see the `MathFunctions` library listed in the dependencies, and we can choose to build the project before the test application is built.

A review – running and debugging your application

You'll spend a lot of time editing, compiling, and debugging your code in Qt Creator, so it's wise to remember the following basics:

- The arrow key runs your application without the debugger; to debug your application, choose the arrow key with the bug icon on it.

- You can switch between the **Editor** view and the **Debug** view of your application by clicking on the **Edit** or **Debug** view choice on the left-hand side; if you debug your application, Qt Creator will enter the **Debug** view automatically.

- There's more to breakpoints than just stopping at a line of code! Use data breakpoints to pin down weird bugs that occur only sometimes or to quickly skip over the first bazillion items of a large loop.

- The variable pane lets you see more than just the contents of variables; you can also add expressions composed of several variables and arithmetic or view arbitrary memory locations.

- Want to hack around a bug during a debugging session? You can change the values of variables in the variable pane and continue running, changing the program's state as you go.

Summary

Qt Creator's Integrated Development Environment contains an editor and tools to start the compiler, linker, and debugger in order to build and debug your applications. Using this, you can start and stop your application, place breakpoints while your application is stopped, or examine the variables or the logical flow of your application.

While Qt Creator manages most of the project for you, sometimes you just have to get down and dirty with a .pro file. You can use scopes to handle conditional compilation (things such as when building for a specific platform or whether a file should be included in the **Release** or **Debug** mode). The .pro file consists of scopes, variables, and their values; by setting the variables that the .pro file feeds qmake, qmake understands the dependencies in your project and magically creates a make file to build your application.

In the next chapter, we'll move on from the mechanics of making a project build and take a look at Qt Creator's UI designer as well as give you a brief introduction to the worlds of Qt Widgets and Qt Quick.

3
Designing Your Application with Qt Designer

Qt is perhaps best known as a cross-platform user interface toolkit, and only in the last few years has Qt Creator really evolved to be a full software development environment. Even in its early releases, however, Qt had an excellent facility for building user interfaces with Qt Designer, now part of Qt Creator. More recently, the developers building Qt have added Qt Quick as a second option for user interface development. Qt Quick extends the Qt libraries and Qt Designer capabilities of Qt Creator to build fluid interfaces for touch screens and set-top boxes. This is facilitated by the declarative nature of Qt Quick and **Qt Meta-Object Language (QML)**.

In this chapter, we will cover:

- Qt's notion of signals and slots
- Creating user interfaces with Qt Designer
- How to instantiate forms, messages, and dialogs
- Introduce Qt Quick's support for declarative UI development

At the end of this chapter, you'll be well equipped to decide whether your application should be written using Qt Widgets or Qt Quick, and to build your application with the help of the documentation that accompanies Qt Creator.

Code interlude – signals and slots

In software systems, there is often the need to couple different objects. Ideally, this coupling should be loose, that is, not dependent on the system's compile-time configuration. This is especially obvious when you consider user interfaces, for example, a button press might adjust the contents of a text widget, or cause something to appear or disappear. Many systems use events for this purpose; components offering data encapsulate that data in an event, and an event loop (or more recently, an event listener) catches the event and performs some action. This is known as **event-driven** programming or the event model.

Qt offers signals and slots as the interface it uses to manage events. Like an event, the sending component generates a signal—in Qt parlance, the object emits a signal, which is an occurrence of an event—which recipient objects may execute a slot for the purpose. Qt objects might emit more than one signal, and signals might carry arguments; in addition, multiple Qt objects can have slots connected to the same signal, making it easy to arrange one-to-many notifications.

Qt provides a macro, `connect`, that lets you connect signals to slots. Equally important is the fact that if no object is interested in a signal, it can be safely ignored and no slots will be connected to the signal. Equally important, if no slots are connected to a signal, it will simply be ignored. Any object that inherits from `QObject`, Qt's base class for objects, can emit signals or provide slots for connection to signals. Under the hood, Qt provides extensions to C++ syntax to declare signals and slots.

A simple example will help make this clear. The classic example you find in the Qt documentation is an excellent one, and we'll use it again here, with some extension. Imagine that you have the need for a counter, that is, a container that holds an integer. In C++, you might write something like the following block of code:

```
class Counter
{
public:
  Counter() { m_value = 0; }

  int value() const { return m_value; }
  void setValue(int value);

private:
  int m_value;
};
```

The Counter class has a single private member, m_value, bearing its value. Clients can invoke value to obtain the counter's value, or set its value by invoking setValue with a new value.

In Qt, we can write the class this way, using signals and slots:

```
#include <QObject>

class Counter : public QObject
{
  Q_OBJECT

public:
  Counter(QObject *parent = 0) : QObject(parent),  m_value(0) {
  }


  int value() const { return m_value; }

public slots:
  void setValue(int value);
  void increment();
  void decrement();

signals:
  void valueChanged(int newValue);

private:
  int m_value;
};
```

This Counter class inherits from QObject the base class for all Qt objects. To make all the functionality of QObject (such as the signal-slot mechanism) available, subclasses of QObject must include the declaration Q_OBJECT as the first element of their definition; this macro expands to the Qt code, implementing the subclass-specific glue necessary for the Qt object and signal-slot mechanism. The constructor remains the same, initializing our private member to 0. Similarly, the accessor method value remains the same, returning the current value for the counter.

An object's slots must be public and are declared using the Qt extension to C++ public slots. This code defines three slots: a setValue slot, which accepts a new value for the counter, and the increment and decrement slots, which increment and decrement the value of the counter. Slots might take arguments, but must not return them; the communication between a signal and its slots is one way: initiating with the signal and terminating with the slot(s) connected to the signal.

The counter offers a single signal. Signals are also declared using a Qt extension to C++ signals. A Counter object emits the valueChanged signal a single argument, which is the new value of the counter. A signal is a function signature, not a method; Qt's extensions to C++ use the type signature of signals and slots to ensure type safety between signal-slot connections, a key advantage signals and slots have over other decoupled messaging schemes.

As developers, it's our responsibility to implement each slot in our class with whatever application logic makes sense. The Counter class's slots look like this:

```cpp
void Counter::setValue(int newValue)
{
  if (newValue != m_value) {
      m_value = newValue;
      emit valueChanged(newValue);
  }
}

void Counter::increment()
{
  setValue(value() + 1);
}

void Counter::decrement()
{
  setValue(value() - 1);
}
```

We use the implementation of the setValue slot as a method, which is what all slots are at their heart. The setValue slot takes a new value and assigns the new value to the private member variable of Counter if they aren't the same. Then, the signal emits the valueChanged signal, using the Qt extension emit, which triggers an invocation to the slots connected to the signal.

This is a common pattern for signals that handle object properties: testing the property to be set for equality with the new value and only assigning and emitting a signal if the values are unequal.

If we had a button, say, QPushButton, we could connect its clicked signal to the increment or decrement slot so that a click on the button increments or decrements the counter. I'd do this using the QObject::connect method, like this:

```
QPushButton* button = new QPushButton(tr("Increment"), this);
Counter* counter = new Counter(this);
QObject::connect(button, SIGNAL(clicked(void)),
                 counter, SLOT(increment(void)));
```

We first create the QPushButton and Counter objects. The QPushButton constructor takes a string, the label for the button, which we denote to be the Increment string or its localized counterpart.

Why do we pass this to each constructor? Qt provides a parent-child memory management between the QObject objects and their descendants, easing cleanup when you're done using an object. When you free an object, Qt also frees any children of the parent object so that you don't have to. The parent-child relationship is set at construction time; I signal to tell the constructors that when the object invoking this code is freed, PushButton and counter can be freed as well. (Of course, the invoking method must also be a subclass of QObject for this to work.)

Next, I call QObject::connect, passing first the source object and the signal to be connected and then the receiver object and the slot to which the signal should be sent. The types of the signal and slot must match and the signals and slots must be wrapped in the SIGNAL and SLOT macros, respectively.

Signals can be connected to signals too, and when this happens, the signals are chained and trigger any slots connected to the downstream signals. For example, I can write:

```
Counter a, b;
QObject::QObject::connect(&a, SIGNAL(valueChanged(int)),
                 &b, SLOT(setValue(int)));
```

This connects the b counter with the a counter so that any changes in value to the a counter also change the value of the b counter.

There's also `disconnect`, which breaks the connection between a signal and a particular slot. Invoking disconnect is similar to invoking connect:

```
disconnect(&a, SIGNAL(valueChanged(int)), &b,
    SLOT(setValue(int)));
```

This disconnects the connection we made in the previous example.

Signals and slots are used throughout Qt, both for user interface elements and to handle asynchronous operations such as the presence of data on network sockets, HTTP transaction results, and so forth. Under the hood, signals and slots are very efficient, boiling down to function dispatch operations, so you shouldn't hesitate to use the abstraction in your own designs. Qt provides a special build tool, the meta-object compiler, which compiles the extensions to C++ and is required for signals and slots. It generates the additional code necessary to implement the mechanism.

Creating forms in Qt Designer

Let's create a simple calculator application using Qt Designer and two forms: one form that takes the arguments for an arithmetic operation and a second dialog form to present the results. I'll do this twice in this chapter, first to show you how to do this using Qt Widgets and second by using Qt Quick. The example is contrived, but will show you how to create multiple user interface forms in both environments and give you practice in working with signals and slots.

 F1 is the keystroke you can use in Qt Creator to get help. As you write code in this and subsequent chapters, any class or method you're curious about, select it and hit *F1*. You'll be taken to Qt's `Help` mode, with documentation about that class or method.

Creating the main form

In *Chapter 1, Getting Started with Qt Creator*, you learned the basic elements of the Qt Widgets designer, including the palette of widgets you can use, the central **Edit** pane, the tree of objects, and the **Property** view. The following screenshot shows the Qt Designer again:

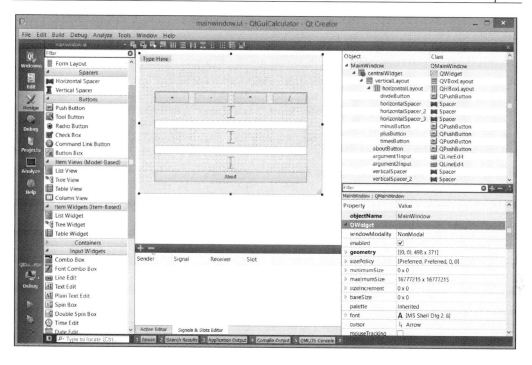

Working from left to right, the parts of the screen you see are:

- The **Views** selector, presently indicating that the Qt Designer view is active.

- The palette of possible widgets you can lay out on your form.

- The form editor, above the connection editor that lets you wire signals and slots between widgets.

- The object tree, indicating all of the objects that have been laid out on the form and showing their parent-child relationships through the use of nested lists.

- Below the object tree is the **Property** editor, where you can edit the compile-time properties of any item you select on the form editor.

Let's begin by creating a new Qt Widgets project (Qt Widgets Application from the **New File or Projects...** dialog) and naming the project QtGuiCalculator, and then, follow these steps:

1. In the Forms folder of the project, double-click on the mainwindow.ui file. The designer will open.

2. Drag out a vertical layout from the palette.

3. Right-click on the layout and choose **Lay out**, then choose **Adjust Size...**. The layout will shrink to a point.

4. Drag two line editors and drop them on the vertical layout in the object viewer (the far right pane). You'll see the vertical layout grow to accept each of the line editors. You should now have something that looks like the following screenshot, where the layout now has two text fields:

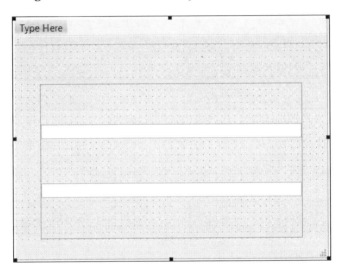

5. Drag a horizontal layout and drop it on the vertical layout in the object viewer.

6. Drag and drop four **Push** buttons on the horizontal layout you just added.

7. Resize the containing window so that the entire layout shows in the window.

8. Rename the buttons, `plusButton`, `minusButton`, `timesButton`, and `divideButton`, using the **Property** browser in the lower-right area of the screen. As you do so, scroll down to the **text** property (under **QAbstractButton**) and give each button a logical label such as +, -, *, and /.

9. Select the top line input and name it `argument1Input`.

10. Select the bottom input line and name it `argument2Input`.

The next screenshot shows what you should see in the Qt Designer form editor pane so far. You can also manually arrange the buttons by breaking the layout and positioning them using the mouse, but that typically makes your layout less robust to window resizing and is generally not a good idea. The following screenshot depicts our calculator user interface:

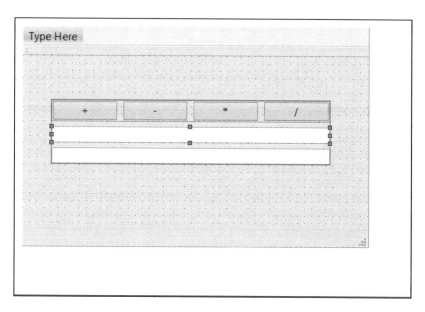

So far, this is pretty straightforward. We used a vertical layout and a horizontal layout to lay out the various controls; this takes advantage of Qt's dynamic constraints on widget layout and sizing. All widgets have minimum and maximum size properties, which are used by layouts to determine the actual size a widget consumes. Some widgets are elastic; that is, they stretch to fill their contents. When specifying the actual size of a widget, you can specify that it takes one of the following values in each of the x and y axes:

- The minimum size of the widget
- The maximum size of the widget
- A fixed size between its minimum and maximum
- An expanding size, expanding to fit the contents of the widget

Qt provides four kinds of layouts, which you can mix and match as we just did. You've encountered the vertical and horizontal layouts; there's also a grid layout, which lets you organize things in an m x n grid, and a form layout, which organizes widgets in a manner similar to how the native platform enumerates fields on a form.

Right now, our layout's a little bunched up. Let's add some spacers to better fill the space in the window and also add a button for an about box:

1. Drag a vertical spacer and drop it between the input lines and a second vertical spacer between the horizontal layout that contains the row of buttons and the input line.

2. Drag a **Push** button to the vertical layout and add a spacer between the bottom line and the **Push** button.

3. Name the last **Push** button `aboutButton` and give it the text `About`. We'll add an icon later.

The next screenshot shows the application as we've constructed it in the designer if you click on the **Run** button.

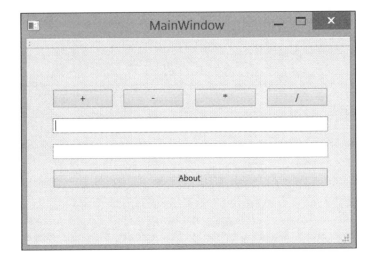

Now, let's make our result dialog. Right-click on the project and choose **Add New...**; then follow these steps:

1. In the dialog that appears, choose **Qt** on the left and then **Qt Designer Form** in the middle. Click on **Choose**.

2. Choose a dialog style for your dialog; choose **Dialog with Buttons Bottom** and click on **Next**.

3. Name the file `resultdialog.ui` and click on **Next**.

4. Click on **Finish**.

5. In the dialog that appears, drag out a form layout. Right-click on it and choose **Lay out and Adjust size**.

6. Add a label to the form layout. Change its text to read `Result`.

7. Drag out another label and name it `result`. In the `objectName` field under `Property`, change the name to `result`.

You should have a dialog that looks like the following screenshot:

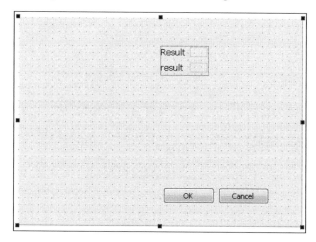

Now is a good time for you to experiment with layouts and spacers and style the dialog any way you wish.

Using application resources

Now, let's add an icon to the application for the **About** button. You can draw one or go to a website like The Noun Project (`http://thenounproject.com/`) for a suitable icon. Icons can be PNG, JPEG, or other formats; a good choice is SVG, because SVG images are vector-based and scale correctly to different sizes. Put the resource file in your project directory and then perform the following steps:

1. Choose the **Edit** view in Qt Creator.

2. Right-click on the project, then choose **Add New....** In the **New File** dialog that opens, click on **Qt** under **Files and Classes** and click on **Qt Resource file**.

3. Name the file `resources`.

4. Add it to the current project.

5. If `resources.qrc` isn't already open in the editor, double-click on it in the solution pane. The resource file editor will appear.

6. Click on **Add**, choose **Add prefix**, and make the prefix /.

7. Click on **Add** again, then on **Add Files**, and choose your icon.

Icons are loaded in the read-only segment of your application through the Qt resource compiler. You can access them anywhere you'd access a file by prefixing the path and name of the resource with a colon. For example, we might place a text file in our application resources and then open the file for reading like this:

```
QFile file(":/data/myfile.txt");
file.open(QIODevice::ReadOnly | QIODevice::Text);

while (!file.atEnd()) {
  QByteArray line = file.readLine();
  process_line(line);
}
```

Application resources are suitable for text and small media files such as icons or images. However, you should avoid using them for larger items such as movies and large sounds, because they'll needlessly bloat the size of your application binary. For these purposes, it's better to package media files with your application and load them directly from the disk.

In the next section, we'll use the resource you added, when we add our about box to the application.

Instantiating forms, message boxes, and dialogs in your application

Qt Designer generates an XML-based layout file (which ends in .ui) for each form you create in Designer. At compile time, Qt Creator compiles the layout into a header file that constructs the components for your user interface layout. The pattern typically used by Qt applications is to construct a private layout class that the main class instantiates. Here's how it works for the main window:

```
#ifndef MAINWINDOW_H
#define MAINWINDOW_H

#include <QMainWindow>

namespace Ui {
  class MainWindow;
}

class MainWindow : public QMainWindow
```

```
{
    Q_OBJECT

public:
    explicit MainWindow(QWidget *parent = 0);
    ~MainWindow();

private:
    Ui::MainWindow *ui;
};


#endif // MAINWINDOW_H
```

In `mainwindow.cpp`, we have:

```
#include "mainwindow.h"
#include "resultdialog.h"
#include "ui_mainwindow.h"
#include <QMessageBox>

MainWindow::MainWindow(QWidget *parent) :
    QMainWindow(parent),
    ui(new Ui::MainWindow),
{
    ui->setupUi(this);
}
```

Why is the constructor declared explicitly? This prevents the C++ compiler from providing implicit casts so that callers can't use anything but the `MainWindow` instances when referring to `MainWindow`. Qt provides this by default.

The `Ui::MainWindow` class is automatically constructed by Qt Designer; by including its declaration in `mainwindow.cpp`, we create an instance of it and assign that instance to the `ui` field. Once initialized, we call its `setupUi` function, which creates the entire user interface you sketched out in Qt Designer.

The controls we laid out in Qt Designer are accessible as field names. For example, we can modify mainwindow.cpp to invoke an about box by adding a slot to mainwindow.h to handle the case when you click on the about button, and then we can add the code to invoke an about box in the implementation of the slot. To do this, follow these steps:

1. Add a public slot declaration to mainwindow.h, along with a slot named aboutClicked. It should now read like the following code:

```
class MainWindow : public QMainWindow
{
    Q_OBJECT

public:
    explicit MainWindow(QWidget *parent = 0);
    ~MainWindow();

public slots:
    void aboutClicked();

private:
    Ui::MainWindow *ui;
};
```

2. At the top of mainwindow.cpp, add an include statement for the QMessageBox class:

```
#include <QMessageBox>
```

3. Add the implementation of the aboutClicked slot to mainwindow.cpp. This code constructs QMessageBox on the stack and sets its icon to the icon you added in your resources earlier, the text of the dialog to Lorem ipsum, and the title of the message box to About. The exec method of the QMessageBox invocation opens the message box and blocks the application flow until you dismiss the message box. It should read something like the code that follows:

```
void MainWindow::aboutClicked()
{
    QMessageBox messageBox;
    messageBox.setIconPixmap(QPixmap(":/icon.png"));
    messageBox.setText("Lorem ipsum.");
    messageBox.setWindowTitle("About");
    messageBox.exec();
}
```

4. In the `MainWindow` constructor, connect the signal from the `About` button to the slot you just created. Your constructor should now read:

```
MainWindow::MainWindow(QWidget *parent) :
    QMainWindow(parent),
    ui(new Ui::MainWindow),
{
    ui->setupUi(this);
    QObject::connect(ui->aboutButton, SIGNAL(clicked()),
                     this, SLOT(aboutClicked()));
}
```

If we build the application, we now have a fully functioning about box, including the application icon you chose. The `connect` call is just like the previous signal-slot connections we've seen; it connects the clicked signal of the main window UI's `aboutButton` to your `aboutClicked` slot.

A word on naming signals and slots before we continue: a signal is typically named a verb in its past tense, denoting the semantics of the event that just occurred that it's trying to signal. A slot should somehow match those semantics, preferably including more detail as to how the signal is being handled. So, Qt names the button's clicked signal logically, and I expand on this by giving a slot named `aboutClicked`. Of course, you can name your signals and slots whatever you like, but this is a good practice to follow.

Before we wire up the other buttons and implement our calculator logic, we need to set up the class for our results dialog. Qt creates this class automatically using the **user interface compiler (uic)**, which compiles forms into classes. We'll follow the pattern of the `MainWindow` class, creating a private `ui` member that contains an instance of the compile-time generated object that constructs the UI for the results dialog. You can create the `ResultDialog` class using the **New File** wizard available by right-clicking on the project; choose **C++ Class** and name it `ResultDialog`. The class itself should inherit from `QDialog`. The header file should look like this:

```
#ifndef RESULTDIALOG_H
#define RESULTDIALOG_H

#include <QDialog>

namespace Ui {
    class Dialog;
}

class ResultDialog : public QDialog
```

```
{
    Q_OBJECT
public:
    explicit ResultDialog(QWidget *parent = 0);
    ~ResultDialog();

private:
    Ui::Dialog *ui;

};

#endif // RESULTDIALOG_H
```

The first thing we need to do is forward declare the Dialog class created by
Qt Designer; we do this in the Ui namespace, so it doesn't conflict with any other
code in the application. Then, we need to declare a pointer to an instance of that
class as a private member variable; we name this pointer ui, as was done for the
MainWindow class.

You can guess what our ResultDialog implementation looks like:

```
#include "resultdialog.h"
#include "ui_resultdialog.h"

ResultDialog::ResultDialog(QWidget *parent) :
    QDialog(parent),
    ui(new Ui::Dialog)
{
    ui->setupUi(this);

}

ResultDialog::~ResultDialog()
{
    delete ui;
}
```

At construction time, it makes an instance of our Ui:Dialog class and then invokes
its setupUi method to create an instance of the user interface at runtime.

Wiring the Qt Widgets' application logic

The application logic for the calculator is simple: we add a property setter to ResultDialog that lets us set the result field of the dialog, and then we wire up some arithmetic, signals, and slots in MainWindow to do the actual computation and show the dialog.

First, make the following change to ResultDialog:

```
void ResultDialog::setResult(float r)
{
    ui->result->setText(QString::number(r));
}
```

This method takes a float, the value to show in the dialog, and formats the result as a string using Qt's default formatting. Qt is fully internationalized; if you do this in English-speaking locales, it will use a decimal point, whereas if you do it with a locale set to a region where comma is used as the decimal separator, it will use a comma instead. The number method is a handy one, with overloads taking doubles and floats as well as integers and arguments to indicate the precision and exponentiation of the returned string.

Now, we move on to the modified MainWindow class. First, let's take a look at the revised class declaration:

```
#ifndef MAINWINDOW_H
#define MAINWINDOW_H

#include <QMainWindow>
#include <QPair>

namespace Ui {
    class MainWindow;
}

class ResultDialog;

class MainWindow : public QMainWindow
{
    Q_OBJECT

    typedef QPair<float, float> Arguments;
```

```
public:
    explicit MainWindow(QWidget *parent = 0);
    ~MainWindow();

    Arguments arguments();

signals:
    void computed(float f);

public slots:
    void aboutClicked();
    void plusClicked();
    void minusClicked();
    void timesClicked();
    void divideClicked();

    void showResult(float r);

private:
    Ui::MainWindow *ui;
    ResultDialog* results;
};


#endif // MAINWINDOW_H
```

In addition to the base class QMainWindow, we now include QPair, a simple Qt template that lets us pass pairs of values. We'll use the QPair template, type defined as Arguments, to pass around the pair of arguments for an arithmetic operation.

We add a signal, computed, which the class triggers any time it performs an arithmetic operation. We also add slots for each of the arithmetic button clicks: plusClicked, minusClicked, timesClicked, and dividedClicked. Finally, we add a slot showResult, which shows the result when a computation occurs.

The MainWindow constructor now needs to do a bunch of signal-slot wiring for all of our buttons, signals, and slots. Add the highlighted part of the code in mainwindow.cpp:

```
MainWindow::MainWindow(QWidget *parent) :
    QMainWindow(parent),
    ui(new Ui::MainWindow),
    results(0)
{
    ui->setupUi(this);
```

```
QObject::connect(ui->aboutButton, SIGNAL(clicked()),
                 this, SLOT(aboutClicked()));
QObject::connect(this, SIGNAL(computed(float)),
                 this, SLOT(showResult(float)));
QObject::connect(ui->plusButton, SIGNAL(clicked()),
                 this, SLOT(plusClicked()));
QObject::connect(ui->minusButton, SIGNAL(clicked()),
                 this, SLOT(minusClicked()));
QObject::connect(ui->timesButton, SIGNAL(clicked()),
                 this, SLOT(timesClicked()));
QObject::connect(ui->divideButton, SIGNAL(clicked()),
                 this, SLOT(divideClicked()));
}
```

After connecting the about button to the slot that shows the about dialog, we next connect the computed signal from MainWindow to its showResult slot. Note that this signal/slot carries an argument, which is the value to show. The remaining four connections connect each of the operation buttons with the code to perform a specific arithmetic operation.

The showResult slot creates a new ResultDialog if we don't already have one, sets its result to the incoming value and invokes the dialog:

```
void MainWindow::showResult(float r)
{
    if (!results)
    {
        results = new ResultDialog();
    }
    results->setResult(r);
    results->exec();
}
```

The arguments method is a helper method used by each of the arithmetic functions and fetches the values from each of the input lines, converts them from strings to floating-point numbers, and does a little bit of error checking to ensure that the entries are valid floating-point numbers:

```
MainWindow::Arguments MainWindow::arguments()
{
    bool ok1, ok2;
    float a1 = ui->argument1Input->text().toFloat(&ok1);
    float a2 = ui->argument2Input->text().toFloat(&ok2);
    if (!ok1 || !ok2)
    {
```

```
        QMessageBox messageBox;
        messageBox.setIconPixmap(QPixmap(":/icon.png"));
        messageBox.setText("One of your entries is not a valid
            number.");
        messageBox.setWindowTitle("Error");
        messageBox.exec();
    }
    return Arguments(a1, a2);
}
```

The `toFloat` method of `QString` does just that: converts a string to a floating-point number, returning the number and setting the Boolean value passed in to `true` if the conversion was successful, or `false` if otherwise. The code does this for both argument input lines, then it checks the resulting Boolean values and reports an error if either argument is malformed, before returning a `QPair` class of the arguments to the caller.

The remaining code actually performs the arithmetic, signaling that a computation has occurred when the operation is complete. For example, take the `plusClicked` slot:

```
void MainWindow::plusClicked()
{
    Arguments a = arguments();
    emit computed(a.first + a.second);
}
```

This obtains the arguments from the input lines using the `arguments` function, computes the sum, and then emits the computed signal with the summed value. As we connected the computed signal to the `showResults` slot, this triggers a call to `showResults`, which creates `ResultDialog` if necessary and shows the dialog with the computed result. The `minusClicked`, `timesClicked`, and `divideClicked` methods are all similar.

Learning more about Qt Widgets

There are whole books written about programming with the Qt Widgets widget set; it's a very rich widget set that includes just about everything you'd need to build the average Macintosh, Windows, or Linux application and has the advantage that the UI controls are familiar to most computer users. We'll discuss it more in *Chapter 5, Developing Applications with Qt Widgets*, but you can also consult the Qt documentation at `http://qt-project.org/doc/qt-5/qtwidgets-index.html`.

Code interlude – Qt Quick and the QML syntax

Most of the programming you do at the lowest level is imperative: you describe how an algorithm should work (take this value and square it, search for the first occurrence of this string and replace it, format this data this way, and so forth). With Qt Quick, your programming is largely declarative: instead of saying how, you say what. For example, in C++ with Qt, we might write code like this to draw a rectangle:

```
QRect r(0, 0, 16, 16);
QPainter p;
p.setBrush(QBrush(Qt::blue));
p.drawRect(r);
```

This code creates a rectangle of 16 x 16 pixels, allocates a `QPainter` object that does the drawing, tells the painter that its brush should be colored blue, and then tells the painter to draw the rectangle. In QML, we'd simply write the rectangle as follows:

```
import QtQuick 2.3
Rectangle {
    width: 16
    height: 16
    color: "blue"
}
```

The difference is obvious: we're just saying that there is a blue rectangle that's 16 x 16 pixels. It's up to the Qt Quick runtime to determine how to draw the rectangle.

Qt Quick's underlying language is QML, the Qt Meta-object Language. QML is based heavily on JavaScript, and in fact, most things that you can write in JavaScript, you can also express in QML. Expression syntax is essentially unchanged; assignments, arithmetic, and so forth all are the same and the name/value system is functionally the same, although object frames might be preceded by a type declaration (as you can see with the `Rectangle` example that I just showed you).

A key exception to the *what works in JavaScript works in QML* rule is the lack of a **document object model (DOM)** and things such as the document root for global variables, because there's no root context or DOM on which other things hang. If you're porting a web application to QML, be prepared to refactor those parts of your application's architecture.

Objects in QML must be parented in the fashion of a tree; each QML file must contain an encapsulating object and then can have child objects that have child objects. However, there must be a single root for the hierarchy at the top of the file. Often, this root is a `Rectangle` object, which draws a base rectangle on which its children are presented, or an `Item` object, which is a container for a more complex user interface element that doesn't actually draw anything. Each item can have a name, which is stored in its `id` property.

Most visible QML items can have states, that is, a collection of properties that apply when a particular state is active. This lets you do things such as declare the difference between a button's dormant and pressed state; pressing the button just toggles between the states, and the button's color, shadow, and so on can all change with you not needing to change each individual property.

A key concept in QML that's not present in JavaScript is that of binding: if two QML object properties share the same value, changing one changes the other. Binding couples values with notifications about values; it's similar to how references work in C++, or how pass-by reference works in other languages. This is very handy in coding things like animations, because you can use the value of one object as the value for another object, and when the underlying value changes in one place, both objects are updated.

QML files can depend on each other, or include files of JavaScript for business logic. You've already seen one example of this at the top of every QML file: the import directive instructs the runtime to include the indicated file and version, so when we write `import QtQuick 2.3`, the runtime finds the declaration of the QtQuick module version 2.3 and includes its symbols when parsing the file. This is how you can encapsulate functionality. QML files in your project are included by default, while you can also include JavaScript files and assign them to a specific JavaScript variable.

For example, we can have a JavaScript file `calculatorLogic.js` that implements all of the functionality of our calculator; in the QML, write:

```
import QtQuick 2.3
import "calculatorLogic.js" as CalculatorLogic
Item {
  // someplace in code
  CalculatorLogic.add(argument1, argument2);
}
```

The initial `import` statement loads the JavaScript file and assigns its value to the QML object `CalculatorLogic`; we can then dispatch methods and access properties of that object as if it were any other QML object.

Qt Quick declares a number of basic data types; these match closely with the data types you find in Qt when writing C++ code, although the syntax can differ. Some of the most important types you'll encounter are:

- A point, with the x and y properties.
- A rectangle, with x, y, width, and height properties.
- A size, with width and height properties.
- A color, which is a quoted string in the HTML ARGB notation or a named color from Qt's lexicon of colors. (Most colors you can think of have names in QML.)
- A 2D, 3D, or 4D vector.
- Basic types including Boolean values, strings, integers, and floating-point numbers.

 There are also a lot of visible types for user interface construction; in this chapter, there's only room to touch on a few. For a detailed list of all QML types and the documentation about those types, see `https://qt-project.org/doc/qt-5/qtquick-qmltypereference.html`.

Creating Qt Quick applications in Qt Designer

In *Chapter 1, Getting Started with Qt Creator*, you gained basic familiarity with Qt Designer for Qt Quick applications. Let's have another look before we recreate our calculator app in QML. The next screenshot shows the Qt Designer for Qt Quick window.

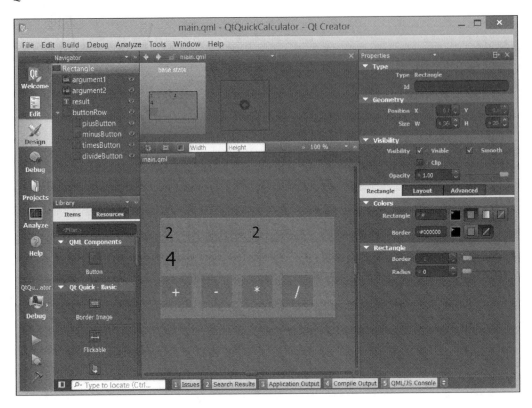

Working from the left again, we have the following components:

- The view selector, showing that the Qt Designer view is active.
- The object hierarchy for the file being edited, showing the parent-child relationship between visible items in that file.
- Below the object hierarchy is a palette of the items you can drag out onto the QML editor pane.

- Next to the object hierarchy is a summary of the states for the object.

- Below the summary of states is the object editor for the QML file.

- Finally, there's a property editor that lets you adjust the properties of the currently selected QML item.

 Personally, I find it easier to just write QML than to use the designer. The syntax takes a little getting used to, but what the designer is good for is previewing the QML you've written by hand and making minor adjustments to its layout.

Speaking of layout, before we see our sample code in detail, it's worth noting that QML has a rich dynamic layout system. Visible items have an anchor property, and you can anchor an item's sides against that of its neighbors or the parent view. You saw this briefly in *Chapter 1, Getting Started with Qt Creator*, where we made a MouseArea object as big as its parent. We'll use that too, to control the layout of the calculator argument input lines and operator buttons.

Let's start making our sample code now by clicking on **New File or Project...** from the **File** menu and walking through the wizard to create a Qt Quick 2.3 application. Name the application QtQuickCalculator.

Creating a reusable button

Our calculator has a button for each operation. While we could make each button a separate rectangle and MouseArea, it's far easier to make a single QML button that encapsulates the behavior of a button, including the change in appearance when you press on it, the placement of the button label, and so forth.

Create a new QML file by right-clicking on the project and choosing **Add New...** and then from the Qt items, choose **QML File (Qt Quick 2)**. The button is a Rectangle object that contains a second Rrectangle object, a Ttext label for the button, and a MouseArea object that handles button clicks. Name the file Button.qml and edit it so that it reads as follows:

```
import QtQuick 2.3

Rectangle {
    id: button

    width: 64
    height: 64
```

```
property alias operation: buttonText.text
signal clicked

color: "green"

Rectangle {
    id: shade
    anchors.fill: button;
    color: "black"; opacity: 0
}

Text {
    id: buttonText
    anchors.centerIn: parent;
    color: "white"
    font.pointSize: 16
}

MouseArea {
    id: mouseArea
    anchors.fill: parent
    onClicked: {
        button.clicked();
    }
}

states: State {
    name: "pressed"; when: mouseArea.pressed == true
    PropertyChanges { target: shade; opacity: .4 }
}
}
```

Working from the top of the code:

- Within the scope of this file, the button's ID is simply button.
- It's 64 pixels in both width and height.
- The button has a single property configurable by its clients, the `operation` property. That property is actually an alias, meaning it's automatically setting the value of the `text` property of `buttonText` instead of being a separate field.
- The button emits a single signal, the `clicked` signal.
- The button's color is green.

- There's a rectangle that fills the button that is colored black, but has an opacity of zero, meaning in normal use it's not visible (transparent). As the button is pressed, we adjust the opacity of this rectangle, to shade the button darker when it's being pressed.

- The text label of the button is 16 points in size, colored white, and centered in the button itself.

- The MouseArea region that accepts clicks for the button is the same size as the button, and it emits the clicked signal.

- The button has two states: the default state and a second state that occurs when the `mouseArea.pressed` property is true (because you are pressing the mouse button in the mouse area). When the state is pressed, we request a single `PropertyChange` property, changing the share rectangle's opacity a bit to give a shadow over the button, darkening it.

You can actually see the two states of the button if you enter Qt Designer, as you can see in the next screenshot. A state is just a name, a when clause indicating when the state is active, and a collection of `PropertyChanges` property indicating what properties should change when the state is active. All visible QML items have a `state` property, which is just the name of the currently active state.

 QML uses signals and slots similar to Qt in C++, but there's no emit keyword. Instead, you declare the signal directly using the signal keyword and the name of the signal, and then you invoke the signal as if it were a function call. For each QML item's signal, the slot is named on and the signal name. Thus, when we use the button, we write an `onClicked` handler for the `clicked` signal. Note that this is different from when writing slots in C++, where you can name a slot anything you want and connect it to a signal with connect.

The calculator's main view

Go back to the editor and edit main.qml directly. We're going to declare our input lines, result line, and four operation buttons directly in code; you can do much of the same with the designer if you'd prefer and then edit the code to match the following:

```
import QtQuick 2.3

Rectangle {
    width: 360
    height: 200
    color: "grey"

    TextInput {
        id: argument1
        anchors.left: parent.left
        width: 160
        anchors.top: parent.top
        anchors.topMargin: 10
        anchors.leftMargin: 10
        anchors.rightMargin: 10
        text: "2"
        font.pointSize: 18
    }

    TextInput {
        id: argument2
        anchors.right: parent.right
        width: 160
        anchors.top: parent.top
        anchors.topMargin: 10
        anchors.leftMargin: 10
        anchors.rightMargin: 10
        text: "2"
        font.pointSize: 18
    }

    Text {
        id: result
        anchors.left: parent.left
        anchors.right: parent.right
        anchors.top: argument2.bottom
        anchors.topMargin: 10
        anchors.leftMargin: 10
```

```
            anchors.rightMargin: 10
            text: "4"
            font.pointSize: 24
        }

    Row {
        id: buttonRow
        anchors.bottom: parent.bottom
        anchors.horizontalCenter: parent
        anchors.bottomMargin: 20
        spacing: 20
        Button {
            id: plusButton
            operation: "+"
            onClicked: result.text =
              parseFloat(argument1.text) +
              parseFloat(argument2.text)
        }

        Button {
            id: minusButton
            operation: "-"
            onClicked: result.text =
              parseFloat(argument1.text) -
              parseFloat(argument2.text)
        }

        Button {
            id: timesButton
            operation: "*"
            onClicked: result.text =
              parseFloat(argument1.text) *
              parseFloat(argument2.text)
        }

        Button {
            id: divideButton
            operation: "/"
            onClicked: result.text =
              parseFloat(argument1.text) /
              parseFloat(argument2.text)
        }
    }
}
```

The view has two text input lines: a read-only text result line and the operation buttons, wrapped in a row item to give them a horizontal layout. The base view for the calculator is gray, which we set with the `color` property, and is in a 360 × 200 pixel window. The controls are positioned as follows:

- The first input line is anchored to the top left of the parent window, with margins of 10 pixels. It's 160 pixels long and has the default height for an 18-point text input field.

- The second input line is anchored to the right side of the parent, with a margin of ten pixels at the top and right. It's also 160 pixels long, and has the default height of an 18-point text input field.

- The result input line's top is anchored to the bottom of the input line and to the left of the parent rectangle. It also has 10 pixels of margins on each side.

- The buttons are spaced 20 pixels apart in a row that's anchored to the bottom of the parent.

These anchors let the view reflow nicely if you resize the application window; the input lines spread across the width of the window, and the button bar on the bottom moves down as the window enlarges.

Each of the buttons has a `click` slot that obtains the floating-point interpretation of each of the input lines and performs the appropriate arithmetic operation. They're each instances of `Button`; the QML class was the class that you wrote in the previous section. Note the use of the JavaScript function, `parseFloat`, in the `onClicked` handlers. As you'd expect from what was mentioned before, there's support for the functions in the JavaScript runtime in QML, so we can just invoke JavaScript functions directly.

The following screenshot shows the completed calculator application. Note that when running the app, if you mouse over a button and press the mouse button, you'll see the shading darken (this isn't shown in the screenshot). This reflects the two states in the button that I showed you in the previous section.

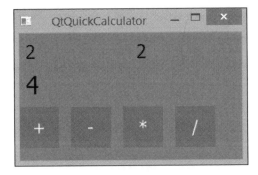

Learning more about Qt Quick and QML

Qt Quick was designed to create fluid applications that don't have a lot of deep widget complexity. Media hubs, photo viewers, phone dialers, web browsers, and other sorts of applications that don't need to match the look and feel of the host platform (or are on embedded systems where the host platform is all written in Qt Quick) are good examples of applications suiting the Qt Quick paradigm.

> For more information about Qt Quick with a plethora of examples that show you the breadth and power of the platform, see `http://qt-project.org/doc/qt-4.8/qdeclarativeexamples.html#touch-interaction`.

Summary

Qt comes with not one, but two complementary GUI toolkits: Qt Widgets, which takes a traditional widget-based approach to GUI development, and Qt Quick, which provides a declarative approach better-suited for platform-agnostic user interfaces for media boxes, some cell phone applications, automobile dashboards, and other embedded environments. For both, Qt offers Qt Designer, a drag-and-drop environment that lets you construct, configure, and preview your user interface as you build your application.

Core to Qt is the notion of signals and slots, Qt's answer to callbacks and events to handle the late-binding required of today's GUI applications. Qt objects can emit signals, which are type-safe function declarations, and other objects can connect to those signals, triggering method calls when the signals are emitted.

In the next chapter, you'll take a break from learning about Qt Creator and graphical user interface development to focus on some fundamental capabilities provided by Qt such as data structures, file I/O, networking with HTTP, and XML parsing.

4
Qt Foundations

Qt is a truly cross-platform framework for building applications. As such, it has a large number of core classes to manage data as well as wrappers around platform services such as threading, the filesystem, network I/O, and of course, graphics.

In this chapter, we discuss some of Qt's core classes that you will find especially handy while writing your applications. In this discussion, we will focus on the bits of Qt that are especially helpful when constructing the business logic for your application. We will begin with a discussion on a handful of useful data classes. After that, we will look at Qt's support for multithreading, a key tool in keeping applications feeling responsive. Next, we will look at file and HTTP I/O, an important component in many applications. We will close with a look at Qt's XML parser, which you can use to create networked applications or use to load XML data from the filesystem.

We will cover the following topics in this chapter:

- Representing data using Qt's core classes
- Multithreading in Qt
- Accessing files using Qt
- Accessing HTTP resources using Qt
- Parsing XML using Qt

Representing data using Qt's core classes

Probably the most common Qt core class you'll run into is `QString`, Qt's container class for character strings. It has similar capabilities to the C++ STL class, `std::wstring`. Like `wstring`, it's multibyte. You can construct one from a traditional C-style `char *` string or another `QString`.

`QString` has lots of helper methods, some of which are as follows:

- `append`: This appends one `QString` class onto another
- `arg`: This is used to build up formatted strings (instead of `sprintf`)
- `at` and `operator[]`: These you can use to access a single character in the `QString`
- `operator==`, `operator!=`, `operator<`, `operator>`, `operator<=`, and `operator>=`: These compare two `QStrings`
- `clear`: This empties a `QString` and sets it to the null string
- `contains`: This searches one string for another string or a regular expression
- `count`: This counts the occurrences of a substring or character in a `QString`
- `startsWith` and `endsWith`: These return true if a `QString` starts with or ends with a specific string, respectively
- `indexOf`: This returns the index of the first occurrence of a substring in a string, or `-1` if the substring doesn't exist in the string
- `insert`: This inserts another `QString` at a specific position in a `QString`
- `lastIndexOf`: This returns the last index of a substring in a `QString`
- `length`: This returns the length of a string in characters
- `remove`: This removes all occurrences or a number of characters of a string from `QString`
- `setNum`: This formats a number and replaces the value of the `QString` with the given number
- `split`: This returns a list of `QString` objects (we'll discuss Qt's lists in a moment) created by splitting the string at a specific separator character
- `toDouble`, `toFloat`, `toInt`, and `toLong`: These return numeric representations of the string if a conversion is possible
- `toLower` and `toUpper`: These return a copy of the string converted to lower- or uppercase
- `truncate`: This truncates the string at a given position

Qt has a number of template collection classes too. The most general of these is QList<T>, which is optimized for fast index-based access as well as fast insertions and deletions. There's also QLinkedList<T>, which uses a linked list structure to store its values, and QVector<T>, which stores its elements in a serial vector array, so the use of template classes is the fastest for indexed access but is slow to resize. Qt also provides QStringList, which is the same as QList<QString> for all intents and purposes.

As you might imagine, these types provide operator[], so you can access and assign any element of the list. Other QList<T> methods you'll find include:

- append: This appends an item to the list
- at: This accesses an individual element of the list for read-only purposes
- clear: This empties the list
- contains: This searches the list for a specific element
- count: This counts the number of times an element occurs in the list
- empty: This returns true if the list is empty
- startsWith and endsWith: These return true if the list begins or ends with the specified element
- first and last: These return the first and last element of the list, respectively
- indexOf: This returns the index of the first occurrence of an item if it's in the list, or -1 if the item's not found
- lastIndexOf: This returns the last index of an item if it's in the list
- length: This returns the length of a list
- prepend: This prepends an item to the list
- push_back and push_front: These push an element to the end or the beginning of the list, respectively
- removeAt, removeFirst, and removeLast: These remove the ith, first, or last element of the list
- replace: This replaces an element of the list
- swap: This swaps two elements of the list at different indices
- toStdList: This returns std::list<T> of the QList
- toVector: This returns QVector<T> of the list

A common thing you'll want to do with a list is iterate over its elements. `QList` provides iterators like the C++ STL does, so you can iterate over the elements of a list like this:

```
QList<QString> list;
list.append("January");
list.append("February");
  ...
list.append("December");

QList<QString>::const_iterator i;
for (i = list.constBegin(); i != list.constEnd(); ++i)
  cout << *i << endl;
```

`QList<T>::const_iterator` and `QList<T>::iterator` provide read-only and mutable iterators over the list; you can obtain one by calling `constBegin` or `begin`, respectively and compare it against `constEnd` or `end` to see when you're at the end of a list.

However, there's an easier way. Qt also provides the `foreach` keyword, which under the hood creates a constant iterator for you. The loop in the previous example can just easily be written as follows:

```
foreach(const QString& string, list)
  cout << string << endl;
```

Similar to a `foreach` keyword in a scripting language, you first specify the variable that contains a reference to each list item in turn and then the list to iterate over. If you're iterating over constant lists, you should prefer the `foreach` keyword, because it's more readable.

Working with key-value pairs

Many a time, you'll want to store key-value pairs, which you might know of as a dictionary or a map if you've used other languages. Qt provides four template classes for this: `QMap`, `QMultiMap`, `QHash`, and `QMultiHash`. They share interfaces, but `QHash` provides faster lookup, although its keys must provide the `==` operator and a global hash function, `qHash()`, as its underlying data structure uses a hash table for its data structure. `QMap`, on the other hand, stores key-value pairs as pairs in a list, so lookups are slower, but you have more flexibility in the key structure you choose. The `QMultiMap` and `QMultiHash` classes let you store multiple values for a single key, while `QMap` and `QHash` only store a single value for each key. Most of the time, it's fine to use `QMap` or `QMultiMap`; it's only if you're managing numbers of keys and values that `QHash` wins out in terms of access performance.

Here's an example of `QMap` with string keys and numeric values:

```
QMap<QString, int> map;
map["one"] = 1;
map["two"] = 2;
map["three"] = 3;
```

You can look up a value with `operator[]` or the `value` method; if you want to check to see whether a value is assigned to a given key, use the `contains` method. One thing to be aware of is that `operator[]` is not quite the same as value; if you use it and no value exists for the given key, it silently inserts a default value with the key you provide, which might not be what you intend. Other methods include:

- `clear`: This clears the dictionary
- `empty`: This returns true if the dictionary is empty
- `insert`: This inserts a key-value pair into the dictionary
- `key`: This returns the first key that matches the value you pass
- `keys`: This returns a list of keys
- `remove`: This removes an element for which you provide the key

All of these container classes, including `QString`, are lightweight: they carry their data by reference when they can and are implemented using copy-on-write. So, let's create an instance of a class and assign it to a second instance, like this:

```
QString oneFish="red fish";
QString twoFish = oneFish;
```

Both `oneFish` and `twoFish` point to the same data under the hood, and only when you begin to change the value of `twoFish` through its methods does it get its own memory buffer. This is an important way in which these classes differ from the STL classes and are key to Qt's better memory performance on low-memory platforms such as mobile devices.

Another lightweight data class you should be aware of is `QByteArray`, which abstracts a collection of bytes in memory for things such as I/O or other data manipulations. You can get a constant `char *` to a `QByteArray` by calling its `constData` method, or a mutable `char *` pointer by calling its `data` method. If you want to know its size, you can call its `length` method. Like `QString`, `QByteArray` has lots of helper functions to search, append data, prepend data, and so forth; so, if you need to manipulate a raw collection of bytes, it's a good idea to look at `QByteArray` before rolling your own implementation with C-style functions.

 For more about these and other Qt core container classes, see `http://qt-project.org/doc/qt-5/containers.html`.

Multithreading in Qt

A **thread** is a single line of execution within a single application. Nearly all of today's operating systems are multithreaded; that is, your application can have more than one concurrent line of execution at a time. Multithreading is a key way to improve the responsiveness of an application, because most processors today can execute multiple threads in parallel and operating systems are optimized to share resources among multiple threads.

Qt supports multithreading over the host operating system through three key classes:

- QThread

- QSemaphore

- QMutex

The first represents a single thread of execution, while the latter two are used to synchronize thread access to data structures.

By design, your application runs entirely on the user thread, a single thread of execution that starts when your application starts. You can create new threads of execution (which cannot manipulate the user interface) by subclassing QThread and overriding the run method. Then, when you need to perform an expensive operation, you just create an instance of your QThread subclass and call its start method. (This is similar to Java, if you're familiar with threading in Java.) In turn, this method calls your run method, and the thread runs until run exits. Once run exits, it emits its completion using the finished signal.

You can connect a slot to that signal to observe task completion. This is especially handy when you use threads to perform background work such as network transactions; you perform the network transaction in the background on the thread, and you'll know when the I/O is complete because your thread will complete and emit the finished method. We will see an example of this in the *Accessing HTTP Resources using Qt* section, later in this chapter.

Here's the simplest of thread examples:

```
class MyThread : public QThread
{
  Q_OBJECT
  void run() Q_DECL_OVERRIDE {
    /* perform the expensive operation */
  }
```

```
};

void MyObject::startWorkInAThread()
{
  MyThread *myThread = new MyThread(this);
  connect(myThread, &MyObject::threadFinished,
          this, MyObject::notifyThreadFinished);
  connect(myThread, &MyThread::finished,
          myThread, &QObject::deleteLater);
  myThread->start();
}
```

Your expensive operation—a computation, file, or network I/O, or whatever—goes in the thread's `run` method. The thread will run as long as `run` is executing; when it's done, it will emit the `finished` signal. To start one of these threads of execution, simply create a new instance of the thread and call its `start` method. You connect two signal handlers to the thread's `finished` method: the first simply deletes the thread when it completes and the second (not shown) updates the UI with the results of the thread's execution.

Multithreaded programming can be tricky, because you need to be aware of cases where one thread is writing to a data structure while another wants to read from the data structure. If you're not careful, you can end up with the reading thread getting garbage, or half-updated data, leading to hard-to-reproduce programming errors. Qt provides two threading primitives to let you block a thread's execution on a resource such as a data structure, letting a thread have exclusive access to that resource while the thread is running: `QMutex` and `QSemaphore`.

A `QMutex` class has two methods:

- `lock`
- `unlock`

To ensure that only one thread has access to a block of code at a time, create a mutex and call its `lock` method. When execution finishes, you must call `unlock`; otherwise, no other thread can run that code. There's also the `tryLock` method, which tries to acquire a lock and immediately returns if it's unable to get the lock in the specified timeout, letting you do something else instead of waiting until your thread gets a lock on the mutex.

QSemaphore is a generalized version of QMutex and lets you manage a pool of *n* items; instead of blocking execution on a single mutex, your thread blocks until it can obtain the number of resources you specify when you invoke its acquire method. When you're done with a number of resources, you call its release method, indicating the number of items you're releasing. QSemaphore also has a tryAcquire method, which immediately returns if the resource acquisition fails in the desired timeout, and an available method, which returns the number of resources presently available.

 Qt 5.3 has also introduced some higher-level programming constructs with Qt Concurrent that are beyond the scope of this book. For more information on QThread and its supporting classes, or Qt Concurrent, consult the Qt documentation at http://qt-project.org/doc/qt-5/threads-technologies.html.

Accessing files using Qt

Files are a specialization of a generalized notion—that of a byte stream that resides somewhere else. Qt encapsulates the more generalized notion of byte streams in its QIODevice class, which is the parent class for QFile as well as network I/O classes such as QTcpSocket. We don't directly create a QIODevice instance, of course, but instead create a subclass such as QFile and then work with the QFile instance directly to read from and write to the file.

 Files and network access usually take time, and thus, your applications shouldn't work with them on the main thread. Consider creating a subclass of QThread to perform I/O operations such as reading from files or accessing the network.

To begin working with a file, we first must open it using the open method. The open method takes a single argument, the manner in which the file should be opened, a bitwise combination of the following:

- QIODevice::ReadOnly: This is used for read-only access
- QIODevice::WriteOnly: This is used for write-only access
- QIODevice::ReadWrite: This is used for read-and-write access
- QIODevice::Append: This is used to only append to the file

- `QIODevice::Truncate`: This is used to truncate the file, discarding all previous contents before writing

- `QIODevice::Text`: This is used to treat the file as text, converting new-line characters to the platform representation during reading and writing

- `QIODevice::Unbuffered`: This is used to bypass any buffering of the input and output

These flags can be combined using the bitwise binary-or operator, `|`. For example, a common combination is `QIODevice::ReadWrite | QIODevice::Text` to read and write a text file. In fact, `QIODevice:ReadWrite` is defined as `QIODevice::Read | QIODevice::Write` internally.

Once you open the file, you can read a number of bytes by calling the file's `read` method and passing the number of bytes to read; the resulting `QByteArray` object contains the data to read. Similarly, you can write `QByteArray` by calling `write`, or use the overloaded `write` method that takes a constant `char *`. In either case, `write` also takes the number of bytes to write. If all you want to do is read the entire contents of a file into a single buffer, you can call `readAll`, which returns `QByteArray` of the entire contents of the file.

Some `QIODevice` subclasses such as `QFile` are seekable; that is, you can position the read/write cursor at any point in the file, or determine its position. You can use the `seek` method to position the cursor at a particular position in the file, and `pos` to obtain the current location of the file cursor. Note that other `QIODevice` subclasses like those for network I/O don't support `seek` and `pos`, but fail gracefully if you attempt to use these methods.

If you want to peek at the data without actually moving the cursor, you can call `peek` and pass the number of bytes to return; the result is a `QByteArray`. Calling `read` after `peek` returns the same data, because `peek` doesn't advance the cursor past the data you've peeked at. The `peek` method is handy when creating a complex parser that needs to know about incoming data in more than one place of its implementation; you can peek at the data, make a decision about how to parse the data, and then call `read` later to get the data.

To determine whether or not you're at the end of a file and there's no more data to read, you can call `atEnd`, which returns true if there is no more data to read. If you want to know how many bytes there are in the file, we can call `bytesAvailable`, which returns the number of bytes available for reading (if known; a network socket might not carry that information, of course).

When working with files, we often need to work with directories as well. The `QDir` class lets us examine the contents of a directory, determine whether a file or directory exists or not, and remove a file or directory. One thing to note is that regardless of the directory separator path used by the host platform, Qt always uses a forward slash / to denote directories, so even if we're writing a Qt program for Windows, we use forward slashes, not back slashes. This makes it easy to write cross-platform compatible code that runs on both Windows and Linux without the need to use special case for the directory handling code.

First, create an instance of `QDir` by passing a file path; after that, you can do the following with it:

- Get an absolute path to the directory by calling `absolutePath`
- Switch to a different valid directory by calling `cd`
- Get a list of files in the directory by calling `entryInfoList`
- Determine whether a specific file or directory exists by calling `exists`
- Determine whether the directory is the root of the filesystem by calling `isRoot`
- Remove a file by calling `remove` and passing the name of the file to `remove`
- Rename a file by calling `rename`
- Remove an empty directory by calling `rmdir` and passing the name of the directory to `remove`
- Compare two directories using the `==` and `!=` operators

Of course, locations of files, such as application preferences and/or temporary files, differ from platform to platform; the `QStandardPaths` class has a static method `standardLocations` that returns a path to the kind of storage we're looking for. To use it, we pass a value from the `QStandardPaths::StandardLocation` enumeration, which has values such as:

- `DesktopLocation`: This returns the desktop directory
- `DocumentsLocation`: This returns the documents directory
- `MusicLocation`: This returns the location of music on the filesystem
- `PicturesLocation`: This returns the location of photos on the filesystem
- `TempLocation`: This returns the path to store temporary files
- `HomeLocation`: This returns the path to the current user's home directory
- `DataLocation`: This returns a path to an application-specific directory for persistent data

- `CacheLocation`: This returns a path to where the application can cache data
- `ConfigLocation`: This returns a path to where the application can store configuration settings

 For more information about files and network IO, see the Qt documentation at `http://qt-project.org/doc/qt-5/io-functions.html`.

Accessing HTTP resources using Qt

A common thing to do in today's networked world is use the **HyperText Transfer Protocol (HTTP)** to access a remote resource or service on the Web. To do this, your application should first use Qt's support to select a bearer network to make the HTTP request, and then, it should use its support for HTTP to make one or more HTTP requests across the network connection that the bearer network service opened.

To begin with, you need to be sure that you include the network module in your Qt declaration by editing your project file to include the following:

```
QT += network
```

Today's computing devices support multiple ways to access the network. For example, an Android tablet can have a built-in 4G wireless wide area network adapter as well as a Wi-Fi radio with multiple network configurations for different access points. The Android platform contains sophisticated code to bring up the appropriate network interface based on the wireless network that provides the best bandwidth at the best cost, or prompts the user to select a desired Wi-Fi network, and so forth. Various Linux distributions have similar features, as does Microsoft Windows and Mac OS X. To encapsulate this functionality, Qt provides the bearer network module, which wraps the platform's underlying support to prompt the user which network connection to use, start a network connection, stop a network connection, and so forth.

If you're writing a networked application, you'll want to use this module to prompt the user before your first attempt to use the network to determine how to connect to the network. The easiest way to do this is with a snippet of code like this:

```
bool OpenNetworkConnection() {
  QNetworkConfigurationManager manager;
  const bool canStartIAP = (manager.capabilities() &
    QNetworkConfigurationManager::CanStartAndStopInterfaces);
  // Is there default access point, use it
  QNetworkConfiguration cfg = manager.defaultConfiguration();
```

```
    if (!cfg.isValid() ||
        (!canStartIAP &&
         cfg.state() != QNetworkConfiguration::Active)) {
      QMessageBox::information(this, tr("Network"), tr(
                                "No Access Point found."));

      return false;
    }

    session = new QNetworkSession(cfg, this);
    session->open();
    return session->waitForOpened(-1);
}
```

This code does the following:

- It creates an instance of the network configuration manager.
- It determines whether the manager can start and stop the network interfaces on the system.
- It gets the default configuration for network connectivity.
- If the default configuration is invalid, or the configuration manager can't start the network configuration and no network connection is up, it pops up a dialog box, indicating that the application cannot start a new network connection and returns false to inform the caller that no network connection was established.
- Otherwise, the code gets a network session configured by the default configuration, opens it, and waits until the connection is opened. Under the hood, the platform might prompt the user for a desired network connection, manage one or more radios, and so forth. Once the session is configured, the network is available for your application to use.

Once you establish a connection to the network, you're able to issue network requests, or create low-level communication for TCP or UDP access.

 Further information about low-level networking will not be discussed in this book; if you're curious, you can see the Qt documentation at http://qt-project.org/doc/qt-5/qtnetwork-index.html.

Performing HTTP requests

Qt provides three key classes to perform HTTP requests: QNetworkAccessManager, QNetworkRequest, and QNetworkReply.

We use the QNetworkAccessManager request to configure the semantics of an HTTP request, configuring things such as proxy servers, as well as to actually issue a request. The easiest thing to do is simply to create one, connect its finished signal to a slot you want to have it call when a request is finished, and then call its get method, like this:

```
mNetManager = new QNetworkAccessManager(this);
connect(mNetManager, SIGNAL(finished(QNetworkReply*)),
        this, SLOT(handleNetFinished(QNetworkReply*)));

// later, when you want to make a request
QNetworkReply *reply = mNetManager->get(
  QNetworkRequest( QUrl( url )));
```

The QNetworkAccessManager class has methods for each of the HTTP methods GET, POST, DELETE, HEAD, and PUT, aptly named get, post, delete, head, and put, respectively. For most transactions to simply fetch data, you'll use get, the standard HTTP method to get a remote network resource. If you want to trigger a remote procedure call through the put method, invoke the QNetworkAccessManager class' put method, passing a QNetworkRequest object and a QByteArray or QIODevice pointer to the data to be put to the server.

> If you need to configure a proxy server as part of your request, you can do so using the setProxy method of QNetworkAccessManager. Note that Qt will configure itself with whatever system the HTTP proxy is by default, so you should only need to override the proxy server settings if you're working with an application-specific proxy server for your application.

The QNetworkAccessManager class uses the QNetworkRequest class to encapsulate the semantics of a request, letting you set HTTP headers that accompany the request by calling its setHeader or setRawHeader methods. The setHeader method lets you set specific HTTP headers such as the User-Agent header, while setRawHeader lets you provide custom HTTP header names and values as QByteArray values.

Once you issue a request, the QNetworkAccessManager class takes over, performing the necessary network I/O to look up the remote host, contact the remote host, and issue the request. When the reply is ready, it notifies your code with the finished signal, passing the QNetworkReply class associated with the request. Using the QNetworkReply class, you can access the headers associated with a reply by calling header or rawHeader, to fetch a standard or custom HTTP header, respectively. QNetworkReply inherits from QIODevice, so you can simply use the read or readAll methods to read from the response as you see fit, like this:

```
void MyClass::handleNetFinished(QNetworkReply* reply)
{
    if (reply->error() == QNetworkReply::NoError) {
        QByteArray data = reply->readAll();
    } else {
        qDebug() << QString("net error %1").arg(reply->error());
    }
}
```

For more information about bearer network configuration, see the Qt documentation at http://qt-project.org/doc/qt-5/bearer-management.html. For more information about all of Qt's support for networking, see the Qt documentation at http://qt-project.org/doc/qt-5/qtnetwork-index.html. There are also some good network samples at http://qt-project.org/doc/qt-5/examples-network.html.

Parsing XML using Qt

Earlier versions of Qt had a number of XML parsers, each suited to different tasks and different styles of parsing. Fortunately, in Qt 5, this has been streamlined; the key XML parser to use is the QXmlStreamReader class (see http://qt-project.org/doc/qt-5/qxmlstreamreader.html for details). This class reads from a QIODevice subclass and reads XML tags one at a time, letting you switch on the type of tag the parser encounters. Thus, our parser looks something like this:

```
QXmlStreamReader xml;
xml.setDevice(input);
while (!xml.atEnd()) {
    QXmlStreamReader::TokenType type = xml.readNext();
    switch(type)
    {
        ... // do processing
```

```
  }
}
if (xml.hasError()) {
  ... // do error handling
}
```

The QXMLStreamReader class reads each tag of the XML in turn, each time its readNext method is called. For each tag read, readNext returns the type of the tag read, which will be one of the following:

- StartDocument: This indicates the beginning of the document

- EndDocument: This indicates the end of the document

- StartElement: This indicates the beginning of an element

- EndElement: This indicates the end of an element

- Characters: This indicates that some characters were read

- Comment: This indicates that a comment was read

- DTD: This indicates that the document type declaration was read

- EntityReference: This indicates that an entity reference that could not be resolved was read

- ProcessingInstruction: This indicates that an XML processing instruction was read

Using XML parsing with HTTP

Let's put together the multithreading, HTTP I/O, and XML parsing with some example code—a worker thread that fetches a flat XML document with unique tags from a remote server and parses selected tags from the XML, storing the results as name-value pairs in a QMap<QString, QString>:

A flat XML file is one with no nested elements, that is, an XML document in the following form:

```
<?xml version="1.0"?>
<document>
  <tag>Value</tag>
  <tag2>Value 2</tag2>
</document>
```

We'll begin with the WorkerThread class header:

```
#include <QMap>
#include <QThread>

class QNetworkAccessManager;
class QNetworkReply;
class QuakeListModel;

class WorkerThread : public QThread
{
  Q_OBJECT

public:
  WorkerThread(QObject* owner);
  void run();

  void fetch(const QString& url);
  void cancel();

signals:
  void error(const QString& error);
  void finished(const QMap<QString, QString>&);

private slots:
  void handleNetFinished(QNetworkReply* reply);

private:
  bool mCancelled;
  QNetworkAccessManager* mNetManager;
  QNetworkReply* mReply;
}
```

This class extends QThread, so it's a QObject. Its slot is private, because it's only used within the scope of this class and not available as part of its public interface. To use one, you create it and call its fetch method, passing the URL to fetch. It does its thing, signaling a successful result passing the dictionary of name-value pairs from the XML via the finished signal, or a string with an error message if the request failed via the error signal. If we start a request and the user wants to cancel it, we simply call the cancel method.

The class carries very little data: a cancellation flag (mCancelled), the QNetworkAccessManager instance it uses to perform the I/O (mNetManager), and the QNetworkReply request from the request (mReply).

Implementing WorkerThread

The implementation of the core of WorkerThread looks like this:

```
void WorkerThread::run()
{
  QXmlStreamReader xml;
  QXmlStreamReader::TokenType type;
  QString fieldName;
  QString value;
  QString tag;
  bool successful = false;
  bool gotValue = false;
  QMap<QString, QString> result;

  xml.setDevice(mReply);
  while(!xml.atEnd())
  {
    // If we've been cancelled, stop processing.
    if (mCancelled) break;

    type = xml.readNext();
    bool got_entry = false;
    switch( type )
    {
      case QXmlStreamReader::StartElement:
        {
          QString tag = xml.name().toString().toLower();
          fieldName = tag;
          gotValue = false;
        }
        break;
      case QXmlStreamReader::Characters:
        // Save aside any text
        if (!gotValue)
        {
          value = xml.text().toString();
          gotValue = true;
        }
        break;
      case QXmlStreamReader::EndElement:
        // Save aside this value
        if (gotEntry && gotValue) {
          result[fieldname] = value;
        }
        gotEntry = false;
        gotValue = false;
```

```
        break;
      default:
        break;
    }
  }

  successful = xml.hasError() ? false : true;

  if (!mCancelled && successful) {
    emit finished(result);
  } else if (!mCancelled) {
    emit error(tr("Could not interpret the server's response."));
  }
}

void WorkerThread::fetch(const QString& url)
{
  // Don't try to re-start if we're running
  if (isRunning()) {
    this->cancel();
  }

  QNetworkReply *reply = mNetManager->get(
    QNetworkRequest(QUrl(url)));

  if (!reply) {
    emit error(tr("Could not contact the server."));
  }
}

void WorkerThread::cancel() {
  mCancelled = true;
  wait();
};

void WorkerThread::handleNetFinished(QNetworkReply* reply)
{
  // Start parse by starting the thread.
  if (reply->error() == QNetworkReply::NoError) {
    if (!this->isRunning()) {
      mReply = reply;
      start();
    }
  } else {
    emit error(tr("A network error occurred."));
    qDebug() << QString("net error %1").arg(reply->error());
  }
}
```

There's a lot of code here (and the full class is shown in the download that accompanies this book!), so let's take it method by method.

- The constructor initializes each of our member fields and connects the finished signal of QNetworkAccessManager to our handleNetFinished slot. (The constructor is omitted here, but is provided in the sample code that accompanies this book.)

- The run method is the heart of the class, responsible for reading and parsing the XML response. We put the read and parse in the run method because it's likely to take the most time, and this way, it can run on a background thread, so it doesn't block the user interface.

The run method does the following:

- Initializes the QXMLStreamReader class with our network response, mReply.
- Loops over the tags found in the XML document it's reading. For each tag:

  - If the tag is a start element, it fetches the name of the tag and notes that it's received a new start element

  - If the tag is a character string, it saves aside the character string and notes that it has a value for a tag

  - If it's the end of an XML element and it has both a name of a tag and a value, it assigns the value of the tag to the named slot in the result hash

  - Once all the tags have been read or an error occurs, the code first tests for an error

  - If the parse wasn't cancelled and was successful, the code emits the finished signal passing the resulting QMap with the names and values from the XML document

  - If the parse encountered an error, the code signals an error

  - The fetch method simply cancels the request if one is pending before making an HTTP GET request on using QNetworkAccessManager

  - The cancel method sets the cancellation flag checked by the run method and waits for the thread to finish, ensuring that cancellation occurs before cancel returns.

  - The handleNetFinished method, invoked by QNetworkAccessManager when the HTTP GET request returns, saves aside the resulting network request and starts the thread to read from the remote server and parse the result. If an error occurs, it signals the error with the error signal and logs the HTTP error message to the debugger console.

Summary

We've covered a lot of ground in this chapter. From data structures to files to networking, you've learned how you can use fundamental Qt core and networking classes to build the backend logic for your application. This information helps you build the business logic in your application.

In the next chapter, we'll start looking at the Qt support to build your presentation logic. We'll take a break from these fundamentals and review the key Qt Widget classes for building desktop applications. You'll learn about the plethora of the basic Qt Widget classes available for your application, how Qt's support for the model-view-controller paradigm works, and finally how to render web content in your application using QWebView, Qt's integrated WebKit-based browser for application development.

5
Developing Applications with Qt Widgets

Qt has a long history in cross-platform GUI development. With controls for all aspects of GUI design that closely mimic the native platform's controls (or in many cases, wrap the native platform's controls), it's a versatile choice for any cross-platform development project. For many people, the best way to get started with Qt Widgets is to fool around in Qt Creator's Designer pane, as we did some in *Chapter 3*, *Designing Your Application with Qt Designer*. If you're the type that likes to read the documentation before you unpack a new toy, this chapter is for you.

In this chapter, you get a whirlwind tour of GUI programming using Qt Widgets. This isn't an exhaustive introduction, but will orient you with Qt Designer and the Qt documentation, letting you have a high-level understanding of what you can do as you set out to build your application. You will learn basic application management, how to create dialogs and error pop ups, and see some of the major GUI elements you can create using the designer.

Next, you will learn how to manage the layout of these GUI elements using Qt's flexible layout system, an important part of application development if you're going to target more than one screen size in your application. After that, you will learn about the model-view-controller paradigm and how it's used in Qt for complex controls such as lists and tree views. The chapter will close with a quick peek at Qt's support for WebKit, which lets you integrate rich web content into your application UI using the QWebView control.

We will cover the following topics:

- The main application along with its menus
- Simple Qt Widgets
- Managing the widget layout with layouts
- MVC programming with Qt
- Render web content using QWebView

Your main application and its menus

In order to use Qt Widgets, you need to do two things. First, you need to ensure that you include the widgets module in your project by adding the following line in your project's .pro file:

```
QT += widgets
```

Second, any file using the Qt Widgets should include the QWidgets header as one of the headers. You might also need to include the header files for individual widgets, such as QButton, QMenuBar, and so forth:

```
#include <QWidgets>
```

Qt provides the QGuiApplication class (a subclass of QCoreApplication) to manage your application's life cycle, including the event loop required by today's GUI platforms. You've already seen QCoreApplication, which we used for our console application in the first chapter.

You probably won't do much with QGuiApplication, but there are two signals it offers that are good for you to know about; these are as follows:

- It emits the applicationStateChanged signal when the application state changes, notifying you as to whether an application is suspended, hidden, inactive, or active. It's a good idea to watch this signal on mobile platforms, where you should do a minimum of processing when your application is hidden or inactive.
- It emits the lastWindowClosed signal when your application's primary or parent window has closed and it's about to exit.

In addition to these signals, QGuiApplication has a few static methods that can come in handy to determine things like the application's display name, whether the locale mode shows the text left-to-right or right-to-left, the platform name, and so forth. For a complete list, see the interface documentation at http://qt-project.org/doc/qt-5/qguiapplication.html, or Qt Creator's Help documentation for QGuiApplication.

The main window of QGuiApplication includes a menu bar into which you can add menu items. On Microsoft Windows, the menu bar is a part of the window; on Mac OS X, it's the menu bar at the top of the screen, while X-Windows-based applications, such as Linux, put them where the window manager dictates. Qt provides the QMenuBar class to implement the functionality of a horizontal menu bar; this class has zero or more QMenu instances associated with it, each corresponding to a single menu (such as **File**, **Edit**, and so forth). Menu items themselves are represented as actions, implemented in Qt as instances of the QAction class. It's easiest to understand the flow if we work bottom up from actions to menus to menu bars.

A QAction class is an abstract user interface action that can be imbedded in Qt Widgets such as menus. An action can have the following properties:

- enabled: This is a Boolean flag indicating whether the action is enabled (selectable) or not
- font: This is used to show any text associated with the action
- icon: This is to represent an action
- iconVisibleInMenu: This is a flag that is used to check whether or not the icon is visible in a menu
- shortcut: This is a keyboard shortcut associated with an action
- text: This is a textual description of the action
- toolTip: This is a tooltip for the action
- visible: This shows whether or not the action is visible

Actions have a triggered signal, which fires when the action is triggered, such as when the user selects the corresponding menu item. (Their properties also have changed signals, so you can monitor when they change, but that's a less common thing to do.) If you need to have an action trigger its events as if it were invoked, call its activate method.

An instance of QMenu groups one or more logically related actions; you can use it as either a pull-down menu, as part of a menu bar, or as a context menu. QMenu provides the following methods you can use to build up a menu hierarchy:

- addAction and removeAction: These methods add and remove a single QAction instance, respectively
- clear: This method removes all actions
- addSeparator: This method adds a menu separator between two actions
- addMenu: This method adds a submenu to a menu

Finally, `QMenuBar` groups all of the drop-down menus; it has the `addMenu` and `insertMenu` methods to add and insert menus after and before their specified menu argument.

 Once you add or insert a menu to a menu bar, you can't remove the menu itself. This is consistent with how most GUIs behave; they don't let you remove menus entirely from the main menu bar.

In practice, all of this is far simpler than it sounds because you can use Qt Creator Designer to build your application menus. By opening up the user interface form for your application's main view (ones based on the main window template, `MainWindow`), you can click on the **Type Here** text and create a new `QMenu` instance. Clicking on the new menu bar instance results in the menu bar dropping down and the first menu item being labeled as **Type Here**. To try this, go back to the Qt Widgets sample application in *Chapter 1, Getting Started with Qt Creator* (or the calculator example in the previous chapter) and try clicking on the menu bar in Qt Designer. Again, typing over the menu item with a label creates a menu action; you can then name the action in the **Property** editor. The following screenshot shows this behavior of Qt Designer:

Once you name an action, you just need to connect its triggered signal to a slot in your application. Typically, we do this in our main window's constructor, like this:

```
MainWindow::MainWindow(QWidget *parent) :
    QMainWindow(parent),
    ui(new Ui::MainWindow)
{
```

```
ui->setupUi(this);
connect(ui->actionAbout, SIGNAL(triggered()),
    this, SLOT(handleAbout()));
}
```

 For more about using menus, see Qt's menu sample at
`https://qt-project.org/doc/qt-5/qtwidgets-`
`mainwindows-menus-example.html`.

Simple Qt Widgets

Playing with the widgets in Qt Creator is the best way to get a feel for what's available, but it's worth commenting on a few of the classes you're likely to use the most. We've already talked about menus; next, let's look at buttons text input, and comboboxes. If you're curious what any of these widgets look like, fire up Qt Designer and make one!

Qt's button classes that implement push buttons, checkboxes, and radio buttons all inherit from the `QAbstractButton` class. You can drag out any of the concrete subclasses of `QAbstractButon` in Qt Creator's Designer or instantiate them programmatically. Through `QAbstractButton`, all buttons have the following properties:

- `checkable`: This is a Boolean flag indicating whether the button has checkbox behavior or not
- `checked`: This indicates whether or not the button is presently checked
- `down`: This is a of type Boolean indicating whether or not the button is currently in the pressed state
- `icon`: This is optional
- `shortcut`: This is an optional key
- `text`: This is an optional label

Buttons offer the following signals that you can wire to slots in your application to detect user input:

- The button emits the `clicked` signal when the button is clicked
- The button emits the `pressed` signal when the button is pressed (that is, receives a mouse or pen down event)
- The button emits a `released` signal when the button is released (that is, receives a mouse or pen up event)
- The button emits the `toggled` signal when it changes the state from checked to unchecked or vice versa

You can group multiple buttons in a parent container, such as a QFrame, to control exclusive behavior; this is how radio buttons work. A good choice of a container is the QGroupBox widget, which frames its contents and provides a title for the collection. By placing multiple buttons such as QRadioButtons in a single QFrame container and ensuring that their autoExclusive property is true (the default for QRadioButtons), clicking one radio button checks that button while unchecking all of the others.

 Don't forget that you should use radio buttons for options that have exclusive behavior (that is, only one item can be selected) and checkboxes for items where multiple items can be selected.

I've mentioned icons twice now, once in discussing menus and once in discussing buttons, without really describing how they work in Qt. Of course, you can manipulate bitmaps directly (we will discuss this further in *Chapter 6, Drawing with Qt*), but for most user interface elements, you need a container that can represent an icon in its various modes and states (such as pressed, released, highlighted, and so forth). In Qt, that container is QIcon.

Using QIcon is easy; you can simply instantiate one from a pixmap or resource. For example, to set a button's icon to a particular image in your application resource, you need only write this:

```
button->setIcon(QIcon(":/icon.png"));
```

Under the hood, the QIcon class creates three additional icons for different states for you, as an icon can be in one of the four modes: normal, active, disabled, or selected. Each of the modes can be in two states: on or off. In addition, QIcon will scale the icon to fit the user interface element the icon is associated with, so you can create icons at the largest resolution your user interface requires and rely on QIcon to do the scaling to fit the various elements of your interface.

Let's move on to text. By far, the most common and easy-to-use text container in Qt Widgets is the QLabel class, which is just a label. QLabel can actually display either text or an image; you set its text using its setText method and its image using its setPixmap or setPicture method. The text can be either plain or rich text; rich text is a subset of the HTML4 markup, so you can do simple things such as have bold text, underlined text, or even hyperlinks. If you use a hyperlink with a QLabel class, you should be prepared to catch a user click by connecting to the label's linkActivated signal, which the label emits if the user clicks on a link, sending the URL for the link as the signal's argument.

By default, labels display left-aligned, vertically centered content; you can change this by calling the label's setAlignment method, or by setting the alignment property in Qt Creator Designer. You can also control word wrapping for a label by setting whether or not word wrapping occurs by calling setWordWrap and passing true to enable word wrap, or false to disable it.

Next in complexity is a text entry; Qt provides the QLineEdit element for a single-line text entry and a QTextEdit for multi-line entry. Editing supports whatever the host platform supports, so you usually get undo and redo, copy and paste, and drag and drop functionalities for free using QLineEdit and QTextEdit.

Let's talk about QLineEdit first, because it's a little simpler. It's a widget that lets the user edit a single line of text. QLineEdit has the following properties, which you can set either using Qt Creator Designer or in the source code:

- alignment: This controls the alignment of the text as it's displayed
- cursorPosition: This indicates the current cursor position
- displayText: This shows the text displayed to the user (which can be different depending on the echoMode property)
- echoMode: This can be used to control password-blanking or conventional input line behavior
- hasSelectedText: This property is true if the text field has selected text
- inputMask: This controls input validation (which I'll say more about in a moment)
- maxLength: This specifies the maximum length of the input line in characters
- placeholderText: This is shown as grayed-out text when the text field is empty
- readOnly: When true, this flag indicates that the text field can't be edited
- selectedText: This contains the currently selected text in the text field
- text: This field contains the entire text of the input line

QLineEdit has the following signals:

- cursorPositionChanged: This is emitted by the line editor when the cursor moves
- editingFinished: This is emitted by the line editor when the user has finished editing a text field and moved focus to the next focusable element
- returnPressed: This is emitted by the line editor when the user presses the *Return* or *Enter* key on the keyboard

- `selectionChanged`: This is emitted by the line editor when the selected text changes
- `textChanged`: This is emitted by the line editor when the text in the field changes, passing the new text of the field
- `textEdited`: This is emitted by the line editor when the user changes the text in the field (not when the text changes programmatically), passing the new text of the field

`QLineEdit` instances can perform input validation; you can go about this in two ways: either by setting an input mask or by providing a validator. Input masks are simple and useful for basic tasks such as validating IP addresses or numeric entry. An input mask is a string of characters that indicates the allowable character class for each position in the string. `QLineEdit` defines the following character classes for input masks:

Character in input mask	Character class
A	An ASCII alphabetic character is required: A-Z, a-z
a	An ASCII alphabetic character is permitted but not required
N	An ASCII alphanumeric character is required: A-Z, a-z, 0-9
n	An ASCII alphanumeric character is permitted but not required
X	Any character that is required
x	Any character is permitted but not required
9	An ASCII digit is required: 0-9
0	An ASCII digit is permitted but not required
D	An ASCII digit is required: 1-9
d	An ASCII digit is permitted but not required (1-9)
#	An ASCII digit or plus/minus sign is permitted but not required
H	A hexadecimal character is required: A-F, a-f, 0-9
h	A hexadecimal character is permitted but not required
B	A binary character is required: 0-1
b	A binary character is permitted but not required
>	All following alphabetic characters are uppercased
<	All following alphabetic characters are lowercased
!	Switch off case conversion
\	Use \ to escape the special characters listed above to use them as separators

For example, you can set an input mask for IP addresses by using the string `000.000.000.000;`. This restricts input to three sets of four numeric digits, bracketed by periods.

For more complex validation tasks, you can specify a validator, which is an instance of a class such as `QIntValidator`, `QDoubleValidator`, or `QRegExpValidator` that `QLineEdit` invokes each time the user changes the text, validating the input. Of these, the most flexible is `QRegExpValidator`, which takes a regular expression and validates the input against the regular expression.

For larger blocks of text, you'll want to use `QTextEdit` instances. Unsurprisingly, `QTextEdit` shares a lot of its interface with `QLineEdit`. Differences include the following:

- You can't mask input for passwords as you might with `QLineEdit`
- If the `acceptRichText` flag of `QTextEdit` is true, the field can accept rich text represented as a subset of HTML4
- The rich text of `QTextEdit` is available as the HTML property, while the parsed text is available as the text property

Finally, there's `QComboBox`, which combines an input line with a drop-down menu to prompt the user with a selection of canned text. As you might imagine, its interface is similar to both menus and input lines; you can append and insert items of text to the combobox using `addItem` and `insertItem`. You'll want to connect to its `highlighted` and `editTextChanged` signals, which it emits when the user selects a menu item or changes the text input line.

Managing the widget layout with layouts

Qt Widgets includes a robust layout system to control the presentation of widgets on the display. In Qt Creator Designer, you can pick from the following layouts:

- `QBoxLayout`: This lays out its view children horizontally or vertically
- `QHBoxLayout`: This lays out its view children horizontally
- `QVBoxLayout`: This lays out its view children vertically
- `QFormLayout`: This lays out pairs of widgets (such as labels and textboxes) side by side and then tiles those pairs vertically, giving the appearance of a form
- `QGridLayout`: This lays out widgets in a grid
- `QStackedLayout`: This shows only a single widget at a time

Using one of these layouts is easy: simply choose the appropriate layout in Qt Creator Designer and drag it to the widget or window you're building. If you're constructing a hierarchy of widgets in the code, you add the widgets to the layout and set the parent widget's layout, like this:

```
QWidget *window = new QWidget();
QPushButton *button1 = new QPushButton("One");
QPushButton *button2 = new QPushButton("Two");
QPushButton *button3 = new QPushButton("Three");

QHBoxLayout *layout = new QHBoxLayout;
layout->addWidget(button1);
layout->addWidget(button2);
layout->addWidget(button3);

window->setLayout(layout);
window->show();
```

Layouts work in conjunction with a widget's sizePolicy and sizeHint properties. These properties provide information to the layout and layout manager about how the widgets should be laid out. The sizePolicy property is an instance of the class QSizePolicy and controls layout preferences to choose between layouts in both the horizontal and vertical directions, offering the following choices in each direction:

- QSizePolicy::Fixed: Here, the widget's sizeHint property is the only size the widget should be
- QSizePolicy::Minimum: Here, the widget's size is the minimum it can be, and there's no advantage to it being larger
- QSizePolicy::Maximum: Here, the widget's size is the maximum size it can be; it can be smaller, but should be no larger
- QSizePolicy::Preferred: Here, the widget's sizeHint property is respected if it can be
- QSizePolicy::Expanding: This is used to indicate that the sizeHint property is a recommendation but that more space can be used if it's available.
- QSizePolicy::MinimumExpanding: This is used to indicate that sizeHint is minimal and sufficient, but that more space can be used if it's available.

Widgets in Qt Widgets have size policies that make sense for the general UI constraints of the target platform, and you typically won't need to change the policy with `QSizePolicy::setVerticalPolicy` or `QSizePolicy::setHorizontalPolicy`.

> Use the layout classes and their defaults as much as you can in your application to ensure cross-platform compatibility and proper layout on screens of different sizes. If you're worrying about individual pixel placement for your widgets, you're likely doing something wrong and will end up with a user interface that doesn't look like what you expect on at least some systems some of the time.

For more information about managing widget layouts with the layout classes, see the Qt documentation at `http://qt-project.org/doc/qt-5/layout.html`.

Model-view-controller programming with Qt

Writing software is an exercise in managing abstractions. The more you can reason abstractly about your software system, the better off you are. A key abstraction that's been around in the GUI world since the 1970s is the **model-view-controller (MVC)** paradigm. I'll discuss MVC briefly here, but there's a lot written about it on the Web, so if it's new to you, you should definitely head over to your favorite search engine and look it up.

In MVC, you divide the code that concerns your user interface into three logical components:

- **Model**: This is responsible for storing the data to show to the user. It's a container of some kind and has no knowledge about your user interface, how things should be drawn, or which events or methods should be triggered by the user when she interacts with your application.
- **View**: This is responsible for drawing the model's contents on the display.
- **Controller**: This is responsible for manipulating the contents of the model in response to individual user actions.

Each of these separate logical components only communicates with the next through well-defined interfaces, like this:

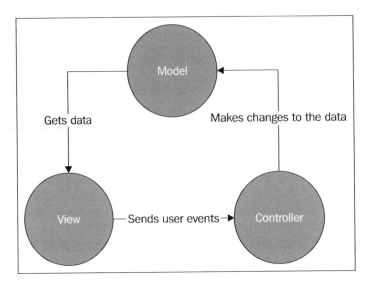

In Qt, the view and controller are combined into simply the view, an arrangement called the **model/view** pattern. To make user interface development as general as possible, Qt also introduces a delegate that makes it easy to switch in and out different user event handlers while sharing the same view and model. Common to both MVC and the model/view pattern is the notion that data and view are separate, which lets you use the same data model for different views, or different models with the same view. Models and their views communicate through signals and slots, as you'd expect.

Qt uses the model/view pattern to manage its more complex user interface elements such as list views, table views, and tree views. The view classes that use Qt's model classes are:

- `QListView`: This shows a sequential list of items
- `QTreeView`: This shows a tree view of items in their hierarchy
- `QTableView`: This shows a table view of items

All of these views accept one of Qt's model classes to store the data Qt presents to the user; these model classes Qt provides all inherit from one of the following abstract base classes:

- `QAbstractItemModel`: This is flexible enough to handle views that present data in the form of tables, lists, and trees

- `QAbstractListModel`: This is a more specialized model superclass optimized to present data in list views

- `QAbstractTableModel`: This is a more specialized model superclass optimized to present data in table views

Most of the time, you don't need to roll your own model for your application. Qt provides several concrete model implementations that are good enough for many applications such as:

- `QStringListModel`: This can be used to store a sequential list of strings

- `QStandardItemModel`: This can be used to store items in an arbitrary tree hierarchy

- `QFileSystemModel`: This can be used as a data model over a filesystem

- `QSqlQueryModel`, `QSqlTableModel`, and `QSqlRelationalTableModel`: These can be used over a SQL database

If these classes don't meet your needs, you can implement a subclass of one of the abstract model classes and hook that to your view. Typically, you'd choose to do this for one of the two reasons: either the existing implementation isn't performant enough for your needs (typically not a problem unless you're managing thousands of items in the model), or you're trying to put a model in front of a new data source other than memory, the filesystem, or SQL.

For example, if you were building a database browser over a MongoDB database, you might want to create a model that queries and updates the MongoDB database directly. If this is an option you need to pursue, be sure to see the Qt documentation on the topic at `http://qt-project.org/doc/qt-5/model-view-programming.html#creating-new-models`.

Analyzing a concrete model subclass

Let's look for a moment at a concrete model subclass and see how you'd move data in and out of it. By far and away, the most common model you'll use is `QStandardItemModel`, which stores its items in as a two-dimensional array of `QStandardItem` instances. Each `QStandardItem` instance can store the following:

- The data associated with the item in the model. This is usually a string, but can also be a number or Boolean value. You access this with the `data` method and set it with the `setData` method.

- The font used to render the item in the view. You access this with the `font` method and set this with the `setFont` method.

- An optional icon associated with the item. You access this with the `icon` method and set this with the `setIcon` method.

- Whether or not the item can be marked with a checkmark, and if so, whether the item is checked. You use the `checkable` and `setCheckable` methods to indicate whether or not the item can be marked and `checked` and `setChecked` to actually set the check state of the item.

- Whether or not the item can be dragged from or dropped to. You use the `dragEnabled`, `dropEnabled`, `setDragEnabled`, and `setDropEnabled` methods to get and set these options.

- Whether or not the item is editable. You use the `editable` and `setEditable` methods to get and set the editable state of the item.

- Whether or not the item is selectable. You use the `selectable` and `setSelectable` methods to get and set the selectable state of the item.

- A tooltip for the item. You use the `toolTip` and `setToolTip` methods to get and set the tooltip for the item.

Each `QStandardItem` method can also have its own rows and columns, giving it the ability to store a tree structure. You can manipulate rows and columns by calling `appendRow`, `appendColumn`, `removeRow`, or `removeColumn`. For example, to create a simple model that represents a tree, you might write:

```
QStandardItemModel model;
QStandardItem *parentItem = model.invisibleRootItem();
for (int i = 0; i < 4; ++i) {
    QStandardItem *item =
        new QStandardItem(QString("node %0").arg(i));
    parentItem->appendRow(item);
    parentItem = item;
}
```

This creates a model with a root element with four child elements, each in their own row. With this model in hand, you can create a tree view that shows the model like this:

```
QTreeView *treeView = new QTreeView(this);
treeView->setModel(myStandardItemModel);
```

Of course, you'll want to know when an item is clicked; the `QTreeView` method emits a clicked signal when the user clicks an item, so you can connect this signal to a slot in your class:

```
connect(treeView, SIGNAL(clicked(QModelIndex)),
        this, SLOT(clicked(QModelIndex)));
```

Qt model/view views use the QModelIndex class to indicate the index of an item into a model; QStandardItem are never passed around between the model and the view. QModelIndex offers the itemFromIndex method to return QStandardItem at the indicated position in the model. Note that you shouldn't cache QModelIndex instances in your application for any length of time, because if the model changes underneath you, the indexes to a given piece of data will change. Similarly, if you need the index of an item in its model, call the item's index method, which returns QModelIndex of the item in the model.

> For more information about Qt's application of the model/
> view pattern, see http://qt-project.org/doc/qt-5/
> model-view-programming.html.

Rendering web content with QWebView

Qt includes a port of WebKit, the popular browser implementation behind Safari and several open source browsers, in its Qt WebKit module. Using the Qt WebKit module, your application can display rich HTML, or even be a full-fledged web browser on its own. It's very easy to create hybrid applications that incorporate both features of native applications as well as displaying web content from local resources, the local filesystem, or the Internet. To use the Qt WebKit module, you must include it in your application by adding the following to your PRO file:

```
QT += webkitwidgets
```

Any source file that accesses the Qt WebKit widgets classes should also include the interfaces with the following #include statement:

```
#include <QtWebKitWidgets>
```

Note that this has changed if you're used to Qt 4.8; in Qt 4.8, the appropriate module to include was simply webkit and the file to include was QtWebKit.

The key class for web page presentation that this module exposes is QWebView; using one is as easy as adding it to a layout in Qt Creator Designer and then telling it to open a document, like this:

```
QWebView *view = new QWebView();
view->load(QUrl("http://www.lothlorien.com/kf6gpe/"));
```

The load method starts the process of firing up the network layer, resolves the URL, fetching the content, and rendering the results. You can also use the setUrl method of QWebView to set its url property, which triggers the same flow, or if you have the HTML locally (say, you built it up programmatically or fetched it from a resource), you can just call its setHtml method.

While QWebView is in the process of loading the page, it emits three signals:

- loadStarted: This is emitted when the page starts to load
- loadProgress: This is emitted for each element of the web view as that element finishes loading
- loadFinished: This is emitted once the page finishes loading

QWebView has the following properties:

- hasSelection: This is true if the user has selected a region in QWebView.
- icon: This is the icon for QWebView.
- selectedHtml: This contains any contents the user has selected in QWebView.
- selectedText: This contains the unmarked-up text the user has selected in QWebView.
- title: This contains the document's title.
- url: This contains the document's URL.
- zoomFactor: This is a real number that indicates how much the page should be zoomed when being rendered. The default value, 1.0, indicates that no scaling should occur.

QWebView contains an instance of QWebPage, available through the page method. The QWebPage method itself is what performs the actual rendering and has one or more QWebFrame instances, one for each frame in the source document. QWebPage has several additional signals you can monitor to observe the behavior of the rendering engine itself:

- loadStarted: This is emitted when QWebPage starts loading the document.
- loadFinished: This is emitted when the QWebPage method finishes loading the page.
- initialLayoutCompleted: This is emitted when QWebPage finishes the initial layout pass on the document.
- pageChanged: This is emitted when QWebPage changes to a new web page.
- urlChanged: This is emitted when QWebPage is about to change its URL before loading a new web page. This signal passes the new URL to the slots connected to the signal.

When you create hybrid applications, you might want to access application data in your C++ application from your application's JavaScript. The QWebPage method provides the addToJavaScriptWindowObject method, which lets you bind a QObject instance to a slot as a child of the web page's window object. For example, let's write the following code snippet:

```
QWebPage *page= myWebPage->page();
page->addToJavaScriptWindowObject(
    "someNameForMyObject", myObject);
```

Properties of your object are available as slots in the exposed object in JavaScript, so you can share data across the C++/JavaScript boundary. The bridge also lets you extend script invocations across the boundary by invoking signal functions on your JavaScript object in JavaScript; this will cause any slots connected to that signal to execute. Similarly, your JavaScript object supports a connect method that lets you connect named slots to JavaScript code, so invoking the signal from C++ invokes the JavaScript methods connected to that slot.

 For more information about QWebView and Qt's support for the WebKit browser, see the Qt documentation at http://qt-project. org/doc/qt-5/qtwebkit-module.html.

Summary

In this chapter, we took a whirlwind tour of the Qt Widgets module. We learned about some of the basic widgets available, and the signals, slots, and properties they provide. We also learned about Qt's application of the MVC paradigm and how for complex widgets like list and tree views, Qt separates concerns into a model and a view, letting us implement new data models for your application, or create new views based on those data models. Finally, we learned about Qt's support for the WebKit browser, letting us build hybrid applications that incorporate the best of JavaScript and HTML with the best of Qt.

In the next chapter, we move on from widgets to low-level drawing, which we can use to either implement our own widgets or basic pixel-based rendering applications.

6
Drawing with Qt

While many applications can be built using only the built-in widgets, others require the ability to perform custom drawing, for example, when you need a custom widget or two, or maybe you're doing offscreen rendering to programmatically create images in graphics files, or else you're interested in building a radically different user interface. Qt provides support for all of these scenarios in C++, in addition to what you can do with Qt Quick.

In this chapter, I will show you what you need to know for general drawing in Qt. We begin by discussing `QPainter` and how it uses `QPaintDevice` instances to abstract drawing functionality. I will show you how this works in general terms and then give concrete examples for offscreen drawing to bitmaps as well as creating custom widgets that interoperate with Qt Widgets. In the last half of the chapter, we will turn to a newer and lower level of abstraction Qt provides for graphics management, the graphics view/graphics scene architecture provided by `QGraphicsView` and `QGraphicsScene`, and how you can use this to build applications in C++ that interoperate with the Qt Widget classes, yet encompassing a complex visual hierarchy.

We will cover the following topics:

- What we need to start drawing with Qt
- Drawing with `QPainter` on `QPaintDevice` instances
- Drawing off screen
- Creating custom widgets
- The Graphics View Framework

Throughout the chapter, don't forget you can always ask for Qt Creator's help for a class or method you find unfamiliar. Qt Creator also comes with a number of examples you can look at; these are in the examples directory under the directory you installed Qt in.

What we need to start drawing with Qt

All the material we cover in this chapter depends on the Qt GUI module, available as part of Qt. Even if you're writing a command-line tool (say, to process image files), you need to include that module in your project by adding the following to your .pro file:

```
QT += gui widgets
```

Of course, in your C++ implementation, we also need to include the header files for the classes we're using. For example, if we're using QImage, QBitmap, and QPainter, be sure to include these headers at the top of your C++ file like this:

```
#include <QImage>
#include <QPainter>
#include <QBitmap>
```

As Qt's painting implementation uses the underlying windowing system, any application that performs graphics operation must be built using QGuiApplication, which initializes the windowing system as part of its startup.

Drawing with QPainter on QPaintDevice instances

At its core, graphics painting requires two things: something that knows how to paint and something that can be painted on. Qt defines the QPainter class as the former and the QPaintDevice as the interface for classes for the latter. You'll seldom instantiate each, but you use both of these classes a lot if you're doing graphics programming; typically, you'll have an instance of a subclass of QPaintDevice, ask it for its associated QPainter, and then use QPainter to perform your drawing. This can happen when you're writing a widget; you'll be passed a QPainter subclass, for example, when you need to paint the widget's contents.

There are several subclasses of QPaintDevice:

- QWidget: This class and its subclasses are used by the widget hierarchy
- QImage: This is a container class for offscreen images that are optimized for input/output and individual pixel access
- QPixmap: This is a container class for offscreen images that's highly optimized for interaction with the screen

- QBitmap: This is a subclass of QPixmap that has a bit depth of 1, making it suitable for monochrome images
- QPicture: This is a paint device that records QPainter drawing operations and can play them back

QPaintDevice subclasses have the width and height methods that return the width and height of the paint device in pixels, respectively; the corresponding widthMM and heightMM methods return the width and height of the paint device in millimeters if known. You can also get the bit depth of the QPaintDevice class by calling its depth method.

We'll discuss further how to get a QPaintDevice subclass in each of the following sections as we see what we want to paint on (say, an offscreen bitmap or a custom widget). Let's turn to QPainter, which is the class we use to perform drawing.

QPainter encapsulates the notion of painting through the use of methods that draw specific shapes (points, lines, polygons, ellipses, arcs, and the like) and a number of settings that control how it performs the actual painting you request. The settings include:

- brush: This indicates how it should fill shapes
- backgroundMode: This indicates whether the background should be opaque or transparent
- font: This indicates the font it should use when drawing text
- pen: This indicates how it should draw outlines of shapes

You can also specify whether or not you have enabled a view transform, which lets you set the affine transforms that the QPainter instance will apply as it performs your drawing.

> Qt lets you specify an arbitrary coordinate system for your QPainter instance that might differ in terms of scale, rotation, and origin from the coordinate system of the target QPaintDevice class. In doing so, it lets you specify the affine transformation between the drawing coordinate system as either a transformation matrix or by separate scale, rotation, and origin offset arguments. The default is no transformation, as you'd expect.
>
> Discussing this is beyond the scope of this section; for more details, see the Qt documentation on this topic at http://qt-project.org/doc/qt-5/qpainter.html#coordinate-transformations.

The QBrush and QPen classes both take QColor instances to specify colors; using QColor, you can specify colors as RGB, HSV, or CMYK values, or by the color's name as one of the colors defined by SVG color name (see a list at http://www.december.com/html/spec/colorsvg.html). In addition to color, QBrush instances also specify a style, a gradient, and a texture; QPen instances specify a style, width, brush, cap style (used on the pen's endpoints), and join style (used when two strokes are joined). Both have simple constructors that set the various fields of the object, or you can specify them through the setter and getter methods. For example, we can create a green pen that is 3 pixels wide and made up of a dashed line with rounded caps and joins, using the following line of code:

```
QPen pen(Qt::green, 3, Qt::DashLine, Qt::RoundCap, Qt::RoundJoin);
```

Similarly, to create QBrush that fills with solid green, you can write this:

```
QBrush brush(Qt::green, Qt::SolidPattern);
```

QFont operates similarly, but of course, there are more options for fonts than for brushes or pens. Typically, you pass the font family to the constructor for the font you want, along with the font size and weight. Qt has a robust font-matching algorithm that attempts to match the desired font family with what's actually available on the system, because it's notoriously hard to predict which fonts are available everywhere once you move away from the common staple of Times New Roman, Helvetica, and so forth. Consequently, the font you get might not be exactly the font you request; you can get the information about a font by creating a QFontInfo method from QFont you create, like this:

```
QFont serifFont("Times", 10);
QFontInfo serifInfo(serifFont);
```

Once you set the brush, pen, and font of QPainter, drawing is simply a matter of calling the various QPainter methods. Rather than enumerating all of them, I'll direct your attention to just a few and then show you an example that uses some of them:

- drawArc: This draws an arc starting at an angle and spanning an angle in a rectangle. Angles are measured in sixteenths of a degree.
- drawConvexPolygon: This takes a list of points and draws a convex polygon.
- drawEllipse: This draws an ellipse in a rectangle (to draw a circle, make the rectangle a square).
- drawImage: This draws an image (QImage), taking the target rectangle, the image, and the source rectangle.
- drawLine: This draws a single line; drawLines draws a series of lines.
- drawPicture: This draws a picture (QPicture).

- drawPixmap: This draws a pixmap (QPixmap).
- drawPoint and drawPoints: These draw a point or an array of points.
- drawPolygon: This draws a (possibly concave) polygon, giving its points as either an array of points or in QPolygon.
- drawPolyline: This draws a polyline.
- drawRect: This draws a single rectangle; drawRects draws multiple rectangles.
- drawText: This draws a text string.
- fillPath: This fills a polygonal path with the brush you pass.
- fillRect: This draws a filled polygon with the brush you pass.

To facilitate these methods, Qt defines helper container classes including QPoint, QLine, and QPolygon. These take integer coordinates; if you want a greater position when drawing (say, when drawing with a transform), you can use the floating point variants, QPointF, QLineF, and QPolygonF.

Let's see how all of this stacks up in practice by drawing a face. Given a QPainter class, we can write:

```
// painter is the QPainter instance we use for painting.
QPen pen(Qt::black, 2, Qt::SolidLine);
QBrush whiteBrush(Qt::white, Qt::SolidPattern);
QBrush blackBrush(Qt::black, Qt::SolidPattern);
QRect faceOutline(0, 0, 100, 100);
painter.setPen(pen);
painter.setBrush(whiteBrush);
painter.drawEllipse(faceOutline);
QRect mouth(30, 60, 40, 20);
painter.drawArc(mouth, 180*16, 180*16);
QRect eye(25, 25, 10, 10);
painter.setBrush(blackBrush);
painter.drawEllipse(eye);
eye = QRect(65, 25, 10, 10);
painter.drawEllipse(eye);
QPoint nosePoints[3] = {
  QPoint(50, 45),
  QPoint(40, 50),
  QPoint(50, 50) };
painter.drawPolyline(nosePoints, 3);
```

This code begins by defining a solid black pen and solid black and white brushes, setting the pen to the pen we created. Next, it creates a square of 100 pixels per side, into which it draws a white circle using `drawEllipse`. After that, we draw the mouth, which is a half-ellipse arc at the bottom of the circle. Next, we draw two eyes, each a filled circle using a single rectangle. Finally, we draw a nose using two lines defined by three points. You can see the result in the following screenshot:

Now, let's see how to use `QPainter` to draw off screen.

Drawing off screen

There are a number of reasons why you might like to draw offscreen: you might want to compose a collection of images and show them one after another (this is called double-buffering, which you can do to avoid screen painting flicker when you draw onscreen), or write a program that generates image files directly.

As I mentioned in the previous section, Qt provides several classes for offscreen drawing, each with different advantages and disadvantages. These classes are `QImage`, `QPixmap`, `QBitmap`, and `QPicture`. Under normal circumstances, you need to choose between `QImage` and `QPixmap`.

QImage is the class best-suited for general-purpose drawing where you're interested in loading the image from or saving the image to a file. If you're working with resources, combining multiple images, and doing a bit of drawing, QImage is the class you want to use.

On the other hand, if you're working primarily with offscreen rendering for the purposes of display performance or double-buffering, you'll want to use `QPixmap`. `QPixmap` is optimized to use data structures and the underlying windowing system and interoperates with the native windowing system more quickly than `QImage`. `QBitmap` is just a convenience subclass of `QPixmap` that defines a monochrome bitmap.

`QPicture` is an interesting beast that records drawing operations in a resolution-independent format that you can save to a file and replay later. You might want to do that if you want to create lightweight platform-independent vector images, but typically just using a PNG format at the appropriate resolution is probably easier.

To get a painter for one of these classes, simply create an instance of the class and then pass a pointer to the instance of a `QPainter` constructor. For example, to perform the drawing in the previous section to an offscreen image and save it to a PNG file, we'd begin by writing:

```
QImage image(100, 100, QImage::Format_ARGB32);
QPainter painter(&image);
```

The first line creates an image that's 100 pixels square, encoding each pixel a 32-bit integer, 8 bits for each channel of opacity, red, green, and blue. The second line creates a `QPainter` instance that can draw on the `QImage` instance. Next, we perform the drawing you just saw in the previous section, and when we're done, we write the image to a PNG file with the line:

```
image.save("face.png");
```

`QImage` supports a number of image formats, including PNG and JPEG. `QImage` also has a `load` method, where you can load an image from a file or resource.

Creating custom widgets

Painting with a custom widget is at its heart no different than offscreen painting; all you need is a widget subclass and a painter pointing to the widget, and you're all set. Yet, how do you know when paint?

Qt's `QWidget` class defines an interface used by the rendering system to pass events to your widget: Qt defines the `QEvent` class to encapsulate the data about an event, and the `QWidget` class defines an interface that Qt's rendering system uses to pass events to your widget for processing. Qt uses this event system not just to indicate things like mouse movements and keyboard input, but also for requests to paint the screen as well.

Let's look at painting first. QWidget defines the `paintEvent` method, which Qt's rendering system invokes, passing a `QPaintEvent` pointer. The `QPaintEvent` pointer includes the region that needs to be repainted and the bounding rectangle of the region, because it's often faster to repaint an entire rectangle than a complex region. When you draw a widget's content with `QPainter`, Qt performs the necessary clipping to the region; however, you can use the information as a hint to what needs to be redrawn if it's helpful.

Let's look at another painting example; this time, an analog clock widget. This example is from the sample code that comes with Qt; you can see it at http://qt-project.org/doc/qt-4.8/widgets-analogclock-analogclock-cpp. html. I've included the whole QWidget subclass implementing an analog clock here. We'll pick through it in several pieces; first come the obligatory header inclusions:

```
#include <QtGui>
#include "analogclock.h"
```

The constructor comes after the header inclusions:

```
AnalogClock::AnalogClock(QWidget *parent)
  : QWidget(parent)
{
  QTimer *timer = new QTimer(this);
  connect(timer, SIGNAL(timeout()), this, SLOT(update()));
  timer->start(1000);

  resize(200, 200);
}
```

The constructor creates a timer object that emits a timeout signal every 1000 milliseconds and connects that timer to the widget's update slot. The update slot forces the widget to repaint; this is how the widget will update itself every second. Finally, it resizes the widget itself to be 200 pixels on a side.

The next part is the paint event handler. This is a long method, so we'll look at it in pieces. Before this is the declaration of stack variables, including the coordinate arrays and colors for the hour and minute hands and getting a QPainter instance with which to paint:

```
void AnalogClock::paintEvent(QPaintEvent *)
{
  static const QPoint hourHand[3] = {
    QPoint(7, 8),
    QPoint(-7, 8),
    QPoint(0, -40)
  };
  static const QPoint minuteHand[3] = {
    QPoint(7, 8),
    QPoint(-7, 8),
    QPoint(0, -70)
  };

  QColor hourColor(127, 0, 127);
  QColor minuteColor(0, 127, 127, 191);
```

```
int side = qMin(width(), height());
QTime time = QTime::currentTime();

QPainter painter(this);
```

Next is the code that sets up the painter itself. We requested an antialiased drawing and use Qt's support to scale and translate the view to make our coordinate math a little easier: we translate the origin to the middle of the widget. Finally, we set the pen and brush: we choose NoPen for the pen, so the only things drawn are fills, and we set the brush initially to the hour brush color:

```
painter.setRenderHint(QPainter::Antialiasing);
painter.translate(width() / 2, height() / 2);
painter.scale(side / 200.0, side / 200.0);

painter.setPen(Qt::NoPen);
painter.setBrush(hourColor);
```

After that, we draw the hour hand. This code uses Qt's support for rotation in rendering to rotate the viewport by the right amount to place the hour hand (each hour takes 30 degrees) and draws a single convex polygon for the hand itself. The code saves the configured state of the painter before doing the rotation and then restores the (unrotated) state after drawing the hour hand:

```
painter.save();
painter.rotate(30.0 * ((time.hour() + time.minute() / 60.0)));
painter.drawConvexPolygon(hourHand, 3);
painter.restore();
```

Of course, hour hands are better read with hour markings, so we loop through 12 rotations, drawing a line for each hour mark:

```
painter.setPen(hourColor);

for (int i = 0; i < 12; ++i) {
  painter.drawLine(88, 0, 96, 0);
  painter.rotate(30.0);
}
```

With the hour hand out of the way, it's time to draw the minute hand. We use the same trick with rotation to rotate the minute hand to the correct position, drawing another convex polygon for the minute hand:

```
painter.setPen(Qt::NoPen);
painter.setBrush(minuteColor);
```

```
painter.save();
painter.rotate(6.0 * (time.minute() + time.second() / 60.0));
painter.drawConvexPolygon(minuteHand, 3);
painter.restore();
```

Finally, we draw 60 tick marks around the face of the clock, one for each minute:

```
painter.setPen(minuteColor);

for (int j = 0; j < 60; ++j) {
if ((j % 5) != 0)
  painter.drawLine(92, 0, 96, 0);
  painter.rotate(6.0);
  }
}
```

As I hinted earlier, custom widgets can also accept events; the mousePressEvent, mouseReleaseEvent, and mouseDoubleClick events indicate when the user presses, releases, or double-clicks on the mouse within the bounds of the widget. There's also mouseMoveEvent, which the Qt system invokes whenever the mouse moves in a widget and a mouse button is pressed down. The interface also specifies events for key presses: there's keyPressEvent that tells you when the user has pressed a key, along with the focusInEvent and focusOut events that indicate when the widget gains and loses keyboard focus, respectively.

The following screenshot shows the clock face in action:

> For more information about the QWidget interface and creating custom widgets, see the QWidget documentation at http://qt-project.org/doc/qt-5/qwidget.html and the Qt event system at http://qt-project.org/doc/qt-5/eventsandfilters.html.

The Graphics View Framework

Qt provides a separate view framework, the Graphics View Framework, to draw hundreds or thousands of relatively lightweight customized items at once. You will choose the Graphics View Framework if you're implementing your own widget set from scratch (although, you might want to consider Qt Quick for this as well), or if you have a large number of items to display on the screen at once, each with their own position and data. This is especially important for applications that process and display a great deal of data, such as geographic information systems or computer-aided design applications.

In the Graphics View Framework, Qt defines the scene, responsible for providing a fast interface to a large number of items. (If you remember our discussion of MVC from the previous chapter, you can think of the scene as the model for the view renderer.) The scene also distributes events to the items it contains and manages the state of individual items in the scene. QGraphicsScene is the Qt class responsible for the implementation of the scene. You can think of QGraphicsScene as a container of drawable items, each a subclass of QGraphicsItem.

Your QGraphicsItem subclass can be used to override the drawing and event handling for each item, and you can then add your custom items to your QGraphicsScene class by calling the addItem method QGraphicsScene. QGraphicsScene offers an items method that returns a collection of items contained by or intersecting with a point, rectangle, a polygon, or a general vector path. Under the hood, QGraphicsScene uses a binary space partitioning tree (see Wikipedia's article on BSP trees at http://en.wikipedia.org/wiki/Binary_space_partitioning) for very fast searching of the item hierarchy by position.

Within the scene are one or more QGraphicsItem subclass instances representing graphical items in the scene; Qt defines some simple subclasses for rendering, but you'll probably need to create your own. Qt provides:

- QGraphicsRectItem: This is used to render rectangles
- QGraphicsEllipseItem: This is used to render ellipses
- QGraphicsTextItem: This is used to render text

QGraphicsItem provides an interface you can override in your subclass to manage the mouse and keyboard events, drag and drop, interface hierarchies, and collision detection. Each item resides in its own local coordinate system, and helper functions provide you with fast transformations between an item's coordinates and the scene's coordinates.

The View framework uses one or more QGraphicsView instances to display the contents of a QGraphicsScene class. You can attach several views to the same scene, each with their own translation and rotation to see different parts of the scene. The QGraphicsView widget is a scroll area, so you can also hook scrollbars to the view and let the user scroll around the view. The view receives input from the keyboard and the mouse, generating scene events for the scene and dispatching those scene events to the scene, which then dispatches those same events to the items in the scene.

The Graphics View Framework is ideally suited to creating games, and in fact, Qt's sample source code is just that: a towers-and-spaceships sample application you can see at http://qt-project.org/wiki/Towers_lasers_and_spacecrafts_example. The game, if you will, is simple, and is played by the computer; the stationary towers shoot the oncoming moving space ships, as you see in the following screenshot:

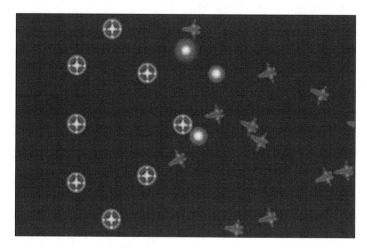

Let's look at bits from this sample application to get a feel of how the Graphics View Framework actually works.

The core of the game is a game timer that updates the positions of mobile units; the application's entry point sets up the timer, QGraphicsView, and a subclass of QGraphicsScene that will be responsible for tracking the state:

```
#include <QtGui>
#include "scene.h"
#include "simpletower.h"

int main(int argc, char **argv)
{
  QApplication app(argc, argv);
  Scene scene;
```

```
    scene.setSceneRect(0,0,640,360);
    QGraphicsView view(&scene);
    QTimer timer;
    QObject::connect(&timer, SIGNAL(timeout()),
    &scene, SLOT(advance()));
    view.show();
    timer.start(10);
    return app.exec();
}
```

The timer kicks over every 10 milliseconds and is connected to the scene's advance slot, responsible for advancing game's state. The QGraphicsView class is the rendering window for the entire scene; it takes an instance of the Scene object from which it's going to render. The application's main function initializes the view, scene, and timer, starts the timer, and then passes control to Qt's event loop.

The Scene class has two methods: its constructor, which creates some non-moving towers in the scene, and the advance method, which advances the scene's one-time tick, triggered each time that the timer in the main function elapses. Let's look at the constructor first:

```
#include "scene.h"
#include "mobileunit.h"
#include "simpletower.h"

Scene::Scene()
: QGraphicsScene()
, m_TicTacTime(0)
{
    SimpleTower * simpleTower = new SimpleTower();
    simpleTower->setPos(200.0, 100.0);
    addItem(simpleTower);

    simpleTower = new SimpleTower();
    simpleTower->setPos(200.0, 180.0);
    addItem(simpleTower);

    simpleTower = new SimpleTower();
    simpleTower->setPos(200.0, 260.0);
    addItem(simpleTower);

    simpleTower = new SimpleTower();
    simpleTower->setPos(250.0, 050.0);
    addItem(simpleTower);
```

```
    simpleTower = new SimpleTower();
    simpleTower->setPos(250.0, 310.0);
    addItem(simpleTower);

    simpleTower = new SimpleTower();
    simpleTower->setPos(300.0, 110.0);
    addItem(simpleTower);

    simpleTower = new SimpleTower();
    simpleTower->setPos(300.0, 250.0);
    addItem(simpleTower);

    simpleTower = new SimpleTower();
    simpleTower->setPos(350.0, 180.0);
    addItem(simpleTower);
}
```

Pretty boring—it just creates instances of the static towers and sets their positions, adding each one to the scene with the addItem method. Before we look at the SimpleTower class, let's look at the Scene class's advance method:

```
void Scene::advance()
{
  m_TicTacTime++;

  // delete killed objects
  QGraphicsItem *item=NULL;
  MobileUnit * unit=NULL;
  int i=0;
  while (i<items().count())
  {
    item=items().at(i);
    unit=dynamic_cast<MobileUnit*>(item);
    if (( unit!=NULL) && (unit->isFinished()==true))
    {
      removeItem(item);
      delete unit;
    }
    else
      ++i;
  }

  // Add new units every 20 tictacs
  if(m_TicTacTime % 20==0)
```

```
  {
    MobileUnit * mobileUnit= new MobileUnit();
    qreal h=static_cast<qreal>( qrand() %
      static_cast<int>(height()) );
    mobileUnit->setPos(width(), h);
    addItem(mobileUnit);
  }

  QGraphicsScene::advance();
  update();
}
```

This method has two key sections:

- The first section deletes any mobile units that have expired for some reason (such as their health dropping to 10). This works by looping over all the items in the scene and testing to see whether each is a MobileUnit instance. If it is, the code tests its isFinished function, and if it's true, removes the item from the scene and frees it.

- The second section runs once every 20 passes through the advance method and creates a new MobileUnit object, randomly placing it on the right-hand side of the display. Finally, the method calls the inherited advance method, which triggers an advance call to each item in the scene, followed by calling update, which triggers a redraw of the scene.

Let's look at the QGraphicsItem subclass of SimpleTower next. First, let's look at the SimpleTower constructor:

```
#include <QPainter>
#include <QGraphicsScene>
#include "simpletower.h"
#include "mobileunit.h"
SimpleTower::SimpleTower()
  : QGraphicsRectItem()
  , m_DetectionDistance(100.0)
  , m_Time(0, 0)
  , m_ReloadTime(100)
  , m_ShootIsActive(false)
  , m_Target(NULL)
  , m_TowerImage(QImage(":/lightTower"))
{
  setRect(-15.0, -15.0, 30.0, 30.0);
  m_Time.start();
}
```

The constructor sets the bounds for the tower and starts a time counter used to determine the interval between the times that the tower fires at oncoming ships.

QgraphicsItem instances do their drawing in their paint method; the paint method takes the QPainter pointer you'll use to render the item, along with a pointer to the rendering options for the item and the owning widget in the hierarchy. Here's the paint method of SimpleTower:

```
void SimpleTower::paint(QPainter *painter, const
  QStyleOptionGraphicsItem *option, QWidget *widget)
{
  painter->drawImage(-15,-15,m_TowerImage);
  if ( (m_Target!=NULL) && (m_ShootIsActive) )
  {  // laser beam
    QPointF towerPoint = mapFromScene(pos());
    QPointF target = mapFromScene(m_Target->pos());
    painter->setPen(QPen(Qt::yellow,8.0,Qt::SolidLine));
    painter->drawLine(towerPoint.x(), towerPoint.y(), target.x(),
      target.y());
    painter->setPen(QPen(Qt::red,5.0,Qt::SolidLine));
    painter->drawLine(towerPoint.x(), towerPoint.y(), target.x(),
      target.y());
    painter->setPen(QPen(Qt::white,2.0,Qt::SolidLine));
    painter->drawLine(towerPoint.x(), towerPoint.y(), target.x(),
      target.y());
    m_ShootIsActive=false;
  }
}
```

The paint method has to draw two things: the tower itself, which is a static image loaded at construction time (drawn with drawImage), and if the tower is shooting at a target, draws colored lines between the tower and the mobile unit targeted by the tower.

Next is the advance method:

```
void SimpleTower::advance(int phase)
{
  if (phase==0)
  {
    searchTarget();
    if ( (m_Target!=NULL) && (m_Time.elapsed()> m_ReloadTime) )
      shoot();
  }
}
```

Each time the scene advances, each tower searches for a target, and if one is selected, it shoots at the target. The scene graph invokes each item's `advance` method twice for each advance, passing an integer, indicating whether the items in the scene are about to advance (indicated when the `phase` argument is 0), or that the items in the scene have advanced (indicated when the `phase` segment is 1).

The `searchTarget` method looks for the closest target within the detection distance, and if it finds one, sets the tower's target pointer to the closest unit in range:

```
void SimpleTower::searchTarget()
{
  m_Target=NULL;
  QList<QGraphicsItem* > itemList = scene()->items();
  int i = itemList.count()-1;
  qreal dx, dy, sqrDist;
  qreal sqrDetectionDist = m_DetectionDistance *
    m_DetectionDistance;
  MobileUnit * unit=NULL;
  while( (i>=0) && (NULL==m_Target) )
  {
    QGraphicsItem * item = itemList.at(i);
    unit = dynamic_cast<MobileUnit * >(item);
    if ( (unit!=NULL) && ( unit->lifePoints()>0 ) )
    {
      dx = unit->x()-x();
      dy = unit->y()-y();
      sqrDist = dx*dx+dy*dy;
      if (sqrDist < sqrDetectionDist)
        m_Target=unit;
    }
    --i;
  }
}
```

Note that we cache a pointer to the targeted unit and adjust its position, because in subsequent frames, the targeted unit will move. Finally, the shoot method, which simply sets the Boolean flag used by paint to indicate that the shooting graphic should be drawn, indicates to the target that it's been damaged. This restarts the timer used to track the time between subsequent shots taken by the timer:

```
void SimpleTower::shoot()
{
  m_ShootIsActive=true;
  m_Target->touched(3);
  m_Time.restart();
}
```

Finally, let's look at the `MobileUnit` class that renders the individual moving space ships in the scene. Firstly, we define the `include` directives and then the constructor:

```cpp
#include "mobileunit.h"
#include <QPainter>
#include <QGraphicsScene>
#include <math.h>

MobileUnit::MobileUnit()
  : QGraphicsRectItem()
  , m_LifePoints(10)
  , m_Alpha(0)
  , m_DirX(1.0)
  , m_DirY(0.0)
  , m_Speed(1.0)
  , m_IsFinished(false)
  , m_IsExploding(false)
  , m_ExplosionDuration(500)
  , m_RedExplosion(0.0, 0.0, 20.0, 0.0, 0.0)
  , m_Time(0, 0)
  , m_SpacecraftImage(QImage(":/spacecraft00") )
{
  m_Alpha= static_cast<qreal> (qrand()%90+60);
  qreal speed= static_cast<qreal> (qrand()%10-5);
  m_DirY=cos(m_Alpha/180.0*M_PI );
  m_DirX=sin(m_Alpha/180.0*M_PI);
  m_Alpha= -m_Alpha + 180.0 ;
  m_Speed=1.0+speed*0.1;
  setRect(-10.0, -10.0, 20.0, 20.0);
  m_Time.start();

  m_RedExplosion.setColorAt(0.0, Qt::white);
  m_RedExplosion.setColorAt(0.2, QColor(255, 255, 100, 255));
  m_RedExplosion.setColorAt(0.4, QColor(255, 80, 0, 200));
  m_RedExplosion.setColorAt(1.0, QColor(255, 255, 255, 0));
}
```

The constructor's a little more complex than that of the stationary units. It needs to set an initial heading and speed for the mobile unit. Then, it sets the bounds for the unit and a timer to control its own behavior. If the unit is disabled, it'll explode; we will draw the explosion with concentric circles in a radial gradient, so we need to set the colors at the various points in the gradient.

Next is the `paint` method, which paints the unit or its explosion if it's been damaged:

```
void MobileUnit::paint(QPainter *painter, const
  QStyleOptionGraphicsItem *option, QWidget *widget)
{
  painter->setPen(Qt::NoPen);

  if (!m_IsExploding)
  {
    painter->rotate(m_Alpha);
    painter->drawImage(-15,-14, m_SpacecraftImage);
  }
  else
  {
    painter->setBrush(QBrush(m_RedExplosion));
    qreal explosionRadius= 8.0 + m_Time.elapsed() / 50;
    painter->drawEllipse(-explosionRadius,
      -explosionRadius, 2.0*explosionRadius, 2.0*explosionRadius);
  }
}
```

This is pretty straightforward: if the unit isn't exploding, it just sets the rotation for the image to be drawn and draws the image; otherwise, it draws the circle explosion with the radial gradient brush we configured in the constructor.

After that is the `advance` method, which is responsible for moving the ship from one frame to the next, as well as tracking the state of an exploding ship:

```
void MobileUnit::advance(int phase)
{
  if (phase==0)
  {
    qreal xx=x();
    qreal yy=y();
    if ( (xx<0.0) || (xx > scene()->width() ) )
    { // rebound
      m_DirX=-m_DirX;
      m_Alpha=-m_Alpha;
    }
    if ( (yy<0.0) || (yy > scene()->height()))
    { // rebound
      m_DirY=-m_DirY;
      m_Alpha=180-m_Alpha;
    }
```

```
    if (m_IsExploding)
    {
      m_Speed*=0.98; // decrease speed
      if (m_Time.elapsed() > m_ExplosionDuration)
        m_IsFinished=true; // is dead
    }
    setPos(x()+m_DirX*m_Speed, y()+m_DirY*m_Speed);
  }
}
```

For simplicity's sake, the `advance` method causes items at the edge of the scene to rebound off of the margins by reversing the direction and orientation. If an item is exploding, it slows down, and if the elapsed time in the timer is longer than the explosion duration, the method sets a flag indicating that the item should be removed from the scene during the next scene advance. Finally, this method updates the position of the item by adding the product of the direction and the speed to each coordinate.

Finally, the `touched` method decrements the health points of the mobile unit by the indicated amount, and if the unit's health points go to zero, starts the explosion timer and sets the explosion flag:

```
void MobileUnit::touched (int hurtPoints)
{
  m_LifePoints -= hurtPoints; // decrease life
  if (m_LifePoints<0) m_LifePoints=0;
  if (m_LifePoints==0)
  {
    m_Time.start();
    m_IsExploding=true;
  }
}
```

For more documentation about the Graphics View Framework, see the Qt documentation at http://qt-project.org/doc/qt-4.8/graphicsview.html.

Summary

In this chapter, we learned how Qt provides the `QPaintDevice` interface and `QPainter` class to perform graphics operations. Using `QPaintDevice` subclasses such as `QWidget`, `QImage`, and `QPixmap`, you can perform onscreen and offscreen drawing. We also saw how Qt provides a separate viewable object hierarchy for large numbers of lightweight objects through the Graphics Scene Framework, supported by the classes `QGraphicsView` and `QGraphicsScene` and the `QGraphicsItem` interface.

In the next chapter, we turn from Qt's support for GUIs in C++ to that of Qt Quick. We'll learn about the fundamental Qt Quick constructs, performing animations and other transitions in Qt Quick, and how to integrate Qt Quick with a C++ application.

7
Doing More with Qt Quick

As you saw in *Chapter 3, Designing Your Application with Qt Designer*, Qt Quick is Qt's declarative environment for application development. Qt Quick is ideal for fluid, animated user interfaces where you're working with touch and mouse events more, and where the style of your application is based on graphical resources instead of the need to mirror the host platform's widget set. Qt Quick provides a number of basic graphical elements and the ability to combine them using a scripting language based on JavaScript, giving you the ability to tap existing skills in web design to create user experiences that are impossible to create entirely in HTML and CSS without a great deal of additional work.

In this chapter, we will take a look at Qt Quick in more detail than we did in *Chapter 3, Designing Your Application with Qt Designer*. I will begin by introducing some fundamental Qt Quick constructs to display shapes, images, and text, as well as how to manage user events. Next, I will introduce Qt Quick's transition framework, essential for creating transitions and animations in a declarative environment. Finally, I will end with some words about how to integrate C++ with Qt Quick, important if you're building a large application that needs to access resources outside what Qt Quick can offer.

The fundamental concepts of Qt Quick

As you saw in *Chapter 3, Designing Your Application with Qt Designer*, Qt Quick enables you to focus on declaring what's visible on the screen and how it should behave, rather than creating objects. Qt Quick uses the **Qt Metaobject Language** (**QML**) to do this, which uses a JavaScript-like syntax and a tree structure to define visible objects and their relationships, as well as script their behavior. Objects have a strict parent-child hierarchy that defines their visual relationship; parent objects contain their children on display.

Objects are placed in Qt Quick's main window using the traditional coordinate system, with (0, 0) in the upper left-hand corner of the display. Child objects can be placed in their parents either using coordinates relative to the upper left-hand corner of the parent or through a flexible system of anchors against object boundaries.

Each item has seven invisible anchor lines: left, horizontalCenter, right, top, verticalCenter, bottom, and baseline. All of these are self-explanatory, except baseline, which corresponds to the line on which text will sit. (For items with no text, Qt defines the baseline to be the same as the top anchor line.) Anchors are relative to other objects; each of the anchor lines is a field in the anchor field, and you can set it to the anchor line of another object. For example, let's write the following:

```
import QtQuick 2.3
import QtQuick.Window 2.2

Window {
  visible: true
  width: 360
  height: 360


  Rectangle {
    id: rect1
    height: 100
    width: 100
    anchors.centerIn: parent
    color: "grey"
  }

  Rectangle {
    id: rect2
    height: 100
    width: 100
    anchors.left: rect1.right
    anchors.top: rect1.top
    color: "black"
  }
}
```

This produces the following output:

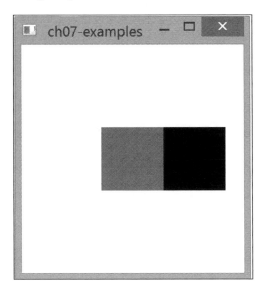

This code creates a window of 360 pixels on a side and two rectangles. Qt places the first rectangle centered in the parent window, and it places the second rectangle to the right-hand side of the first one with the same top lines.

Anchoring doesn't just affect placement, but it can affect sizing too. Consider the following QML:

```
import QtQuick 2.3
import QtQuick.Window 2.2

Window {
  visible: true
  width: 360
  height: 360


  Rectangle {
    id: rect1
    height: 100
    width: 100
    anchors.left: parent.left;
    anchors.verticalCenter: parent.verticalCenter
    color: "grey"
  }
```

```
    Rectangle {
      id: rect2
      anchors.left: rect1.right
      anchors.top: rect1.top;
      anchors.bottom: rect1.bottom
      anchors.right: rect3.left
      color: "black"
    }

    Rectangle {
      id: rect3
      height: 100
      width: 100
      anchors.right: parent.right;
      anchors.verticalCenter: parent.verticalCenter
      color: "grey"
    }
  }
```

This places two squares on either side of the parent window, with a rectangle stretched between the two squares. Note that the anchor.left parameter of rect2 is set to the rect1.right value, and anchor.right of rect2 is set to the rect3.left value. The following screenshot shows how it looks:

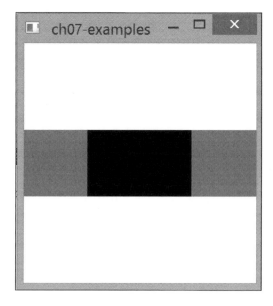

For more complex layouts, Qt Quick defines four positioning elements: Column, Row, Grid, and Flow. These behave much as you'd expect:

- Column: This lays out its children in a vertical column

- Row: This lays out its children in a horizontal strip

- Grid: This lays out its children in a grid

- Flow: This lays out its children side by side, wrapping the elements if necessary

Consider the following Flow element:

```
import QtQuick 2.3
import QtQuick.Window 2.2

Window {
  visible: true
  width: 360
  height: 360

  Flow {
  anchors.fill: parent
  anchors.margins: 4
  spacing: 10

  Rectangle { height: 40; width: 40; color: "grey" }
  Rectangle { height: 40; width: 40; color: "black" }
  Rectangle { height: 40; width: 40; color: "grey" }
  Rectangle { height: 40; width: 40; color: "black" }
  Rectangle { height: 40; width: 40; color: "grey" }
  Rectangle { height: 40; width: 40; color: "black" }
  Rectangle { height: 40; width: 40; color: "grey" }
  Rectangle { height: 40; width: 40; color: "black" }
  Rectangle { height: 40; width: 40; color: "grey" }
  }
}
```

This produces a flow of rectangles from the left to the right, spaced by a margin of ten pixels and with a four-pixel margin on the left-hand side, as follows:

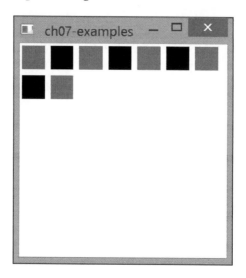

In general, you should use anchoring layouts and the more complex Row, Column, Grid, and Flow elements whenever you don't have total control over the target hardware. Relative-spaced layouts leave Qt making the layout decisions at runtime, so you don't end up with a weird space on big screens or with layouts that overflow the boundaries of small screens. Of course, it takes a little more thought at design time, because you'll need to determine the relative spacing of various items, allocating the maximum space to the items that require it.

Qt Quick defines a number of visible elements besides Rectangle, of course. Visual types include:

- Window: This is the top-level window for an application
- Item: This is the basic visual object type inherited by all visible objects
- Image: This is used to render bitmaps
- AnimatedImage: This is used to play animated GIF images
- AnimatedSprite: This is used to play animated images stored as a sequence of sprites in a single image
- Text: This is used to draw text in a scene

All of these require you to import the QtQuick module, except Window that requires QtQuick.Window. The present version of this module is 2.2, but you can check the documentation for information about specific versions.

Classes such as the `Image` class have a `source` attribute that takes a URL from where it fetches its content. Typically, your images come from either the resource segment of your application or the Web; if you need to load them from other sources or create them dynamically, you can provide an image provider. (I'll show you how to do this in the example at the end of this chapter.)

There's also `WebView`, a control built using Qt WebKit which you can include in your QML, that can render web content. Unlike the other visual elements, you need to import it using `import QtWebKit` to have access to `WebView`. A viewer for a web page in QML is as simple as this:

```
import QtQuick 2.3
import QtQuick.Window 2.2
import QtWebKit 3.0

Window {
  visible: true
  width: 640
  height: 480

  WebView {
    anchors.top: parent.top;
    anchors.left: parent.left
    anchors.right: parent.right;
    anchors.bottom: parent.bottom;
    id: web
    url: "http://www.lothlorien.com"
  }
}
```

Rather than handling user input through event methods, as Qt widgets do, QML defines a collection of objects that accept input. These objects include the following:

- `MouseArea`: This is used for mouse clicks and movement
- `Keys`: This is used for handling keystrokes
- `KeyNavigation`: This is used for handling arrow navigation
- `Flickable`: This is used for handling the flicks of the mouse or touch flicks for scrolling
- `PinchArea`: This is used for handling pinch-to-zoom or other two-fingered interaction
- `MultiPointTouchArea`: This is used for handling generic multi-touch input
- `Drag`: This is used for handling drag-and-drop events for visual items

- `DropArea`: This is used for accepting items dropped from drag areas
- `TextInput`: This is used for capturing free-form text input in a simple input field
- `TextEdit`: This is used for multi-line text input

Each of these defines signals to which you can bind JavaScript, as you saw in *Chapter 3, Designing Your Application with Qt Designer*. For example, `MouseArea` defines the following signals:

- `onClicked`: This is emitted when the user clicks on the mouse area
- `onDoubleClicked`: This is emitted when the user double-clicks on the mouse area
- `onEntered`: This is emitted when the user moves the mouse pointer into the mouse area
- `onExited`: This is emitted when the user moves the mouse pointer out of the mouse area
- `onPressed`: This is emitted when the user presses down on the mouse in the mouse area
- `onReleased`: This is emitted when the user releases the mouse button in the mouse area
- `onWheel`: This is emitted when the user manipulates the mouse scroll wheel in the mouse area

Signals are accompanied by an event containing the specifics of the signal; for example, the `MouseArea` element sends the `MouseEvent` events to the signal handlers. These aren't arguments to the bound JavaScript, but appear as special variables in the JavaScript.

Qt Quick also defines some other views for user interaction that require data models; these are:

- `ListView`: As you can imagine, `ListView` lays out its items in a vertical or horizontal list.
- `GridView`: This lays out its items in `gridPathView`. The `PathView` takes an arbitrary path and lays its items out on the path that you provide.

All these use `ListModel` to contain their data, following the MVC pattern we discussed in the previous chapter. When you do this, you bind the view to the model using the QML's binding, and the view relies on model changes to show the changes in the model. You can provide items for your `ListModel` container in Qt Quick, or supply a subclass of `QAbstractItemModel` and provide your own data through the Qt Quick C++ bindings. (I will discuss how to bind QML and C++ later in this chapter, in the *Integrating Qt Quick and C++* section.) These views are fully touch-enabled, supporting flicks and inertial scrolling. They use the model and a delegate to perform the drawing; the delegate is just a QML `Item` element that references the field in the model. For example, this QML creates a list with three elements, each with two fields: name and number:

```
import QtQuick 2.3
import QtQuick.Window 2.2

Window {
  visible: true
  width: 360
  height: 360

  ListModel {
    id: model
    ListElement {
      name: "Bill Smith"
      number: "555 3264"
    }
    ListElement {
      name: "John Brown"
      number: "555 8426"
    }
    ListElement {
      name: "Sam Wise"
      number: "555 0473"
    }
  }

  ListView {
    model: model
    anchors.top: parent.top;
    anchors.bottom: parent.bottom;
```

```
        anchors.left: parent.left;
        anchors.right: parent.right;
        delegate: Item {
          width: 180
          height: 100
          Column {
            Text { text: name }
            Text { text: number }
          }
        }
      }
    }
```

The `ListModel` container is just that: the list of data for `ListView`. The `ListView` delegate is an `Item` element, with `Column` containing two text fields. Note how the text for each field is just the field name in the `ListModel` fields.

Of course, we can split this in three files. We can save `ListModel` in a file called ContactModel.qml, as follows:

```
// ContactModel.qml
import QtQuick 2.3

ListModel {
  id: model
  ListElement {
    name: "Bill Smith"
    number: "555 3264"
  }
  ListElement {
    name: "John Brown"
    number: "555 8426"
  }
  ListElement {
    name: "Sam Wise"
    number: "555 0473"
  }
}
```

The delegate item cab be saved in a file called ListModelDelegate.qml, as follows:

```
// ListModelDelegate.qml
import QtQuick 2.3
```

```
Item {
    width: 180
    height: 100
    Column {
    Text { text: name }
    Text { text: number }
    }
}
```

Then, our main application will look similar to the following code:

```
import QtQuick 2.3
import QtQuick.Window 2.2

Window {
    visible: true
    width: 360
    height: 360

    ListView {
        model: ContactModel {}
        anchors.top: parent.top;
        anchors.bottom: parent.bottom;
        anchors.left: parent.left;
        anchors.right: parent.right;
        delegate: ListModelDelegate {}
    }
}
```

Dividing up your QML in files is a good idea if you think you'll have a reusable component or when your code gets too long to follow.

States and transitions in Qt Quick

Traditional GUI programming often involves easy-to-write but boilerplate state machines for controls to track control and application states. For example, a button might have several states: when the mouse hovers over it, when it's pressed, and then once pressed, a separate state for on or off in the case of a checkbox or a push button. While this code isn't hard to write, it does involve some writing, and more sophisticated interfaces require more of it.

Qt Quick provides an abstraction for this through its `State` construct, which groups a state's name as well as the condition under which it occurs, and which properties of an object should take on new values. We first saw this in *Chapter 3, Designing Your Application with Qt Designer*, when we wrote our own button component, reprinted here:

```
import QtQuick 2.3

Rectangle {
  id: button

  width: 64
  height: 64

  property alias operation: buttonText.text
  signal clicked

  color: "green"

  Rectangle {
    id: shade
    anchors.fill: button;
    color: "black"; opacity: 0
  }

  Text {
    id: buttonText
    anchors.centerIn: parent;
    color: "white"
    font.pointSize: 16
  }

  MouseArea {
    id: mouseArea
    anchors.fill: parent
    onClicked: {
    button.clicked();
    }
  }

  states: State {
    name: "pressed"; when: mouseArea.pressed == true
    PropertyChanges { target: shade; opacity: .4 }
  }
}
```

Here, the button has two states: the default state in which the shade is fully transparent, and when the user is pressing the button—represented by the pressed state—setting the shade's `opacity` property to `0.4`. The `states` field of an item can actually be an array; another way to write these states is to declare both explicitly, shown as follows:

```
states: [
  State {
    name: "pressed"; when: mouseArea.pressed == true
    PropertyChanges { target: shade; opacity: .4 }
  },
  State {
    name: "released"; when: mouseArea.pressed != true
    PropertyChanges { target: shade; opacity: 0.0 }
  }
]
```

Each `State` construct can have more than one `PropertyChanges` element, each with its own target and property, so you can create sophisticated state transitions using simple declarations.

Qt Quick uses transitions to control the animation of a property when a state change occurs. To create a transition, define an animation; you can apply an animation on any property that can be changed, specifying the start and end values of the animation. Consider a simple animation on a mouse press such as the following:

```
import QtQuick 2.3
import QtQuick.Window 2.2

Window
{
  visible: true
  height: 360
  width: 360

  Rectangle {
    id: rect1
    width: 100; height: 100
    color: "red"

    MouseArea {
      id: mouseArea
      anchors.fill: parent
    }
```

```
      states: State {
        name: "moved"; when: mouseArea.pressed
        PropertyChanges { target: rect1; x: 100; y: 100 }
      }

      transitions: Transition {
        NumberAnimation {
          properties: "x,y"
          easing.type: Easing.InOutQuad
        }
      }
    }
  }
```

Here, the rectangle starts at the origin of the parent coordinate system, with MouseArea in the rectangle. When you press the mouse in the rectangle, the state of the rectangle changes to moved, and the rectangle's top-left corner moves to (100,100) on the parent's canvas. However, we also specify an animation, NumberAnimation, on the x and y properties, so the property change is animated to this value, with the easing curve we specify (a quadratic curve at both the start and finish of the animation).

- There are different animations for different kinds of properties. You can use NumberAnimation to animate numeric properties, as you see here

- There's also ColorAnimation, which animates colors, and RotationAnimation, which animates rotations

Here's the QML to rotate a red rectangle in a half-circle when it's clicked on:

```
import QtQuick 2.3
import QtQuick.Window 2.2

Window
{
  visible: true
  height: 360
  width: 360

  Item {
    width: 300; height: 300
```

```
Rectangle {
    id: rect
    width: 150; height: 100;
    anchors.centerIn: parent
    color: "red"
    antialiasing: true

    states: State {
        name: "rotated"
        PropertyChanges { target: rect; rotation: 180 }
    }

    transitions: Transition {
        RotationAnimation {
            duration: 1000
            direction: RotationAnimation.Counterclockwise
        }
    }
}

MouseArea {
    anchors.fill: parent;
    onClicked: rect.state = "rotated"
}
}
}
```

Again, the pattern is the same: we define a state with `PropertyChanges`, indicating the new property value, and then specify a transition over this property using an animation (in this case, `RotationAnimation`). Here, the transition has a duration specified in milliseconds. Note that the rotation only occurs once, and the rotation angles are bound by the values -360 and 360 degrees.

For more information on the animation and transition framework in Qt Quick, see the Qt Quick documentation at `http://qt-project.org/doc/qt-5/qtquick-statesanimations-animations.html` and the Qt Quick Animation samples at `http://qt-project.org/doc/qt-5/qtquick-animation-example.html`.

Integrating Qt Quick and C++

You can run a simple Qt Quick application using the `qmlviewer` application, an application provided as part of the Qt SDK. However, most of the time, you'll create a Qt Quick application using the Qt Quick application wizard in Qt Creator, which results in a hybrid application consisting of a Qt C++ application container and QML files as resources that the application loads and plays at runtime.

If we take a look at `main.cpp` in a project that we create with this wizard, we will see the following code:

```cpp
#include <QGuiApplication>
#include <QQmlApplicationEngine>

int main(int argc, char *argv[])
{
  QGuiApplication app(argc, argv);

  QQmlApplicationEngine engine;
  engine.load(QUrl(QStringLiteral("qrc:///main.qml")));
  return app.exec();
}
```

This is pretty straightforward: it creates an instance of `QQmlApplicationEngine`, a class that inherits from `QGuiApplication`, and instantiates a top-level window containing a single instance of `QQmlEngine`, the Qt Quick playing engine. Among other things, the `QQmlEngine` class keeps an object called the root context that's a list of all named properties in the QML environment. We can access this root context and add any Qt object to it that we wish.

For example, let's create a native C++ object with a property, shown as follows:

```cpp
#ifndef NATIVEOBJECT_H
#define NATIVEOBJECT_H

#include <QObject>

class NativeObject : public QObject
{
  Q_OBJECT
public:
  explicit NativeObject(QObject *parent = 0) :
  QObject(parent)
  {
```

```
    m_text = "Hello world!";
  }

  Q_PROPERTY(QString text READ text)

  const QString& text() { return m_text; }

private:
  QString m_text;

};


#endif // NATIVEOBJECT_H
```

We can instantiate and bind one of these to the QML engine's root context
when the application starts. To do this, we simply create one and then call the
setContextProperty method of rootContext, passing an instance of our object
and the name to which the engine should bind it, as follows:

```
#include <QGuiApplication>
#include <QQmlApplicationEngine>
#include <QQmlContext>

#include "nativeobject.h"

int main(int argc, char *argv[])
{
  QGuiApplication app(argc, argv);

  QQmlApplicationEngine engine;
  NativeObject object;
  engine.rootContext()->setContextProperty("object",
  dynamic_cast<QObject*>(&object));

  engine.load(QUrl(QStringLiteral("qrc:///main.qml")));

  return app.exec();
}
```

Then, we can access this object using the name `object` anywhere in our QML, as follows:

```
import QtQuick 2.3
import QtQuick.Window 2.2

Window
{
  visible: true
  height: 360
  width: 360

  Text {
  anchors.top: parent.top
  anchors.horizontalCenter: parent.horizontalCenter
  text: object.text
  }
}
```

Here, the `Text` property of our object is dereferenced by the QML engine and used for the text value of the text field in our QML.

This is especially handy for list models; we can create arbitrarily complex models using the filesystem or network resources in C++ and then assign them as the models for the `ListView`, `GridView`, or `PathView` objects, giving us the ability to create a rich user interface in Qt Quick while leveraging Qt's MVC and Qt's flexible network architecture. We'll do this in the next section when we create a custom model to store the image data in a hybrid multimedia capture application.

 For more information about how Qt Quick binds with C++, see the documentation for the `QQmlContext` class at http://qt-project. org/doc/qt-5/qqmlcontext.html and http://qt-project.org/ doc/qt-5/qtquick-modelviewsdata-cppmodels.html.

Putting it all together – an image gallery application

Let's apply what we've discussed in the last few chapters by putting together a simple image gallery application, such as the photo gallery on smartphones. We'll display images from the system's directory in a grid, letting the user flick to scroll the images. Here's how our application will look:

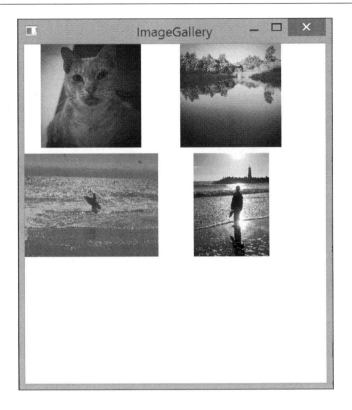

To do this, we need the following components:

- A model containing the paths to the images to be displayed
- A controller responsible for creating the model
- An image provider that can load the images from the system's image directory
- The QML UI

Let's take a look at the application's QML first:

```
import QtQuick 2.3
import QtQuick.Window 2.2

Window {
    visible: true
    width: 1080 / 2
    height: 1920 / 2

    Item {
```

```
        anchors.top: parent.top
        anchors.left: parent.left
        anchors.bottom: parent.bottom
        anchors.right: parent.right
        clip: true

        GridView {
            id: grid
            anchors.fill: parent;
            cellHeight: 190
            cellWidth: 250
            model: ListModel {}
            delegate:  Image {
                width: 240; height: 180
                fillMode: Image.PreserveAspectFit
                source: "image://file/" + path
            }
        }
    }

    Timer {
        interval: 10
        running: true
        repeat: false
        onTriggered: {
            controller.deferredInit()
            grid.model = model
        }
    }
}
```

There's `GridView` with a delegate that uses a single `Image` element to show each element in the gallery. By specifying a URL beginning with `image`, we tell the Qt Quick engine that we want to use a custom image provider; in this case, it is the file image provider that we'll provide at the time of initialization in our `main` function. The images in the grid will be scaled to fit the grid cells, preserving the aspect ratio of the image. The grid begins with an empty list model, which we'll swap for an initialized list model once the timer fires after startup and instructs the controller to initialize the model.

The timer startup is a bit of a hack; the reason for this is that we're going to use a filesystem class that relies on Qt's multithreading to monitor the image directory, and the Qt multithreading system won't be initialized until after we enter the application's main loop. So, we start the main loop, initialize the QML, and then initialize the application controller, which will initialize the model and obtain a list of image files from the directory.

The application's main entry point creates the controller and the model, along with the image provider and binds them to the Qt Quick engine, shown as follows:

```cpp
#include <QGuiApplication>
#include <QQmlApplicationEngine>
#include <QDir>
#include <QQmlContext>

#include "imagegallerycontroller.h"
#include "imagegallerymodel.h"
#include "fileimageprovider.h"

int main(int argc, char *argv[])
{
  QGuiApplication app(argc, argv);
  QQmlApplicationEngine engine;

  ImageGalleryController *controller =
  new ImageGalleryController(&engine);
  ImageGalleryModel *model = controller->model();

  QQmlContext *context = engine.rootContext();
  context->setContextProperty("controller", controller);
  context->setContextProperty("model", model);

  engine.addImageProvider(QLatin1String("file"),
  new FileImageProvider(QQuickImageProvider::Pixmap));
  engine.load( QUrl(QStringLiteral("qrc:///main.qml")));

  return app.exec();
}
```

This code creates an instance of the controller, gets a pointer to the model from the controller, and then binds both of them to the Qt Quick engine. Next, we register an instance of our custom image provider with the engine, saying that anything referred to with the base path of the file should invoke our image provider, fetching pixmaps.

An image provider can either return pixmaps or the QImage instances; pixmaps are slightly faster to draw. The one you return is a function of your image provider; your image provider just loads images or pixmaps from the disk and scales them to fit the display. The following code is used in fileimageprovider.h for this:

```
#ifndef FILEIMAGEPROVIDER_H
#define FILEIMAGEPROVIDER_H

#include <QQuickImageProvider>

class FileImageProvider : public QQuickImageProvider
{
public:
  FileImageProvider(QQuickImageProvider::ImageType type);
  QImage requestImage(const QString& id, QSize* size,
  const QSize& requestedSize);
  QPixmap requestPixmap(const QString& id, QSize* size,
  const QSize& requestedSize);
};

#endif // FILEIMAGEPROVIDER_H
```

Add the following code in a file named fileimageprovider.cpp:

```
#include "fileimageprovider.h"

FileImageProvider::FileImageProvider(
  QQuickImageProvider::ImageType type)  :
  QQuickImageProvider(type)
{
}

QImage FileImageProvider::requestImage(const QString& filename,
  QSize* size, const QSize& requestedSize)
{
  QImage image(filename);
  QImage result;
  if (requestedSize.isValid()) {
    result = image.scaled(requestedSize, Qt::KeepAspectRatio);
  } else {
    result = image;
  }
  *size = result.size();
  return result;
}
```

```
QPixmap FileImageProvider::requestPixmap(const QString& filename,
   QSize* size, const QSize& requestedSize)
{
   QPixmap image(filename);
   QPixmap result;

   if (requestedSize.isValid()) {
      result = image.scaled(requestedSize, Qt::KeepAspectRatio);
   } else {
      result = image;
   }
   *size = result.size();
   return result;
}
```

The image provider interface defines two methods, out of which you need to provide an implementation for at least one. The interface specifies an ID for the image, the desired size of the image, and a pointer to the actual size of the image as your method returns it, and you return either a QImage instance or a pixmap. In this example, I have provided both the implementations to give you an idea of how to do this, although you need to provide only one in your image provider.

 For more information on the interface, see the documentation at http://qt-project.org/doc/qt-5/ qquickimageprovider.html.

Our implementation loads the desired image from the disk as either a pixmap or QImage, and if the caller provides a valid size, resizes the image without changing the aspect ratio. After scaling, we determine the image's size, assign it to the size parameter, and then return the resulting image or pixmap.

Our application is simple such that the sole purpose of the controller is to initialize the data model; so, the controller is a very simple class:

```
#ifndef IMAGEGALLERYCONTROLLER_H
#define IMAGEGALLERYCONTROLLER_H

#include <QObject>

class ImageGalleryModel;
class QAbstractItemModel;

class ImageGalleryController : public QObject
{
```

```
  Q_OBJECT

public:
  explicit ImageGalleryController(QObject *parent = 0);
  ImageGalleryModel* model() const;

signals:

public slots:
  void deferredInit();

private:
  ImageGalleryModel *imageGalleryModel;

};

#endif // IMAGEGALLERYCONTROLLER_H
```

Now, use the following code in `imagegallerycontroller.cpp`:

```cpp
#include <QDir>
#include <QDesktopServices>
#include <QStandardPaths>

#include "imagegallerycontroller.h"
#include "imagegallerymodel.h"

ImageGalleryController::ImageGalleryController(QObject *parent) :
  QObject(parent)
{
  imageGalleryModel = new ImageGalleryModel();
}

ImageGalleryModel *ImageGalleryController::model() const
{
  return imageGalleryModel;
}

void ImageGalleryController::deferredInit()
{
  imageGalleryModel->setRootPath(
  QStandardPaths::standardLocations(
  QStandardPaths::PicturesLocation)[0]);
}
```

There are no surprises here: the controller creates a model on construction, and its deferred initialization sets the root path of the model to the first element in the standard locations for the system's pictures. (This is actually a little risky; some platforms might not have such a directory defined, but it's fine for this example.)

The model is where most of the application's logic resides. First, let's take a look at the model's interface:

```
#ifndef IMAGEGALLERYMODEL_H
#define IMAGEGALLERYMODEL_H

#include <QStandardItemModel>

class QFileSystemWatcher;

class ImageGalleryModel : public QStandardItemModel
{
  Q_OBJECT
public:
  enum ImageGalleryRoles {
  PathRole = Qt::UserRole + 1
  };

  explicit ImageGalleryModel(QObject *parent = 0);

  QHash<int, QByteArray> roleNames() const;
  void setRootPath(const QString& path);
signals:

public slots:
  void onDirectoryChanged(const QString& path);

private:
  QString path;
  QFileSystemWatcher *watcher;
};

#endif // IMAGEGALLERYMODEL_H
```

Each element in a model can store different pieces of data accessed by different roles; we define a single role, PathRole, which will contain the absolute path to a single image. To do this, we need to do two things: define a numeric value for the role (through the ImageGalleryRoles enumeration), and then provide a roleNames method that returns a hash of the role names indexed by the role values. Qt Quick uses the role names in the returned hash to determine how to access individual roles in a single value of the data model: by looking in the hash to find the role name, then getting the role value, and finally by calling the data on the model entry with the desired role.

The model class is the largest class in the application, although even here we use QStandardItemModel to actually do most of the work of the model. Here's the implementation:

```
#include "imagegallerymodel.h"
#include <QDir>
#include <QFile>
#include <QFileSystemWatcher>

ImageGalleryModel::ImageGalleryModel(QObject *parent) :
  QStandardItemModel(parent)
{
  watcher = new QFileSystemWatcher(this);
  connect(watcher, SIGNAL(directoryChanged(QString)),
    this, SLOT(onDirectoryChanged(QString)));
}

QHash<int, QByteArray> ImageGalleryModel::roleNames() const
{
  QHash<int, QByteArray> roles;
  roles[PathRole] = "path";
  return roles;
}

void ImageGalleryModel::setRootPath(const QString &p)
{
  this->clear();

  if (path != "")
  {
    watcher->removePath(path);
  }

  path = p;
```

```
  watcher->addPath(path);

  // Sync the model
  onDirectoryChanged(path);
}

void ImageGalleryModel::onDirectoryChanged(
    const QString &path)
{
  QStringList nameFilters;
  nameFilters << "*.png" << "*.jpg";
  QDir directory(path);
  directory.setNameFilters(nameFilters);
  QStringList files = directory.entryList();

  QHash<QString, int> fileIndexes;

  // Sync the model with the list.

  // Now delete anything in the model not on the filesystem
  for(int i = 0; i < rowCount(); i++)
  {
    QString absolutePath = data(index(i, 0), PathRole)
      .toString();
    QString name = directory.relativeFilePath(absolutePath);
    if (!files.contains(name))
    {
      removeRow(i);
      i--;
      continue;
    }
    fileIndexes[absolutePath] = i;
  }

  // Add anything to the model that's on disk
  // and not in the model
  foreach(const QString &file, files)
  {
    QString absolutePath = directory.absoluteFilePath(file);
    if (!fileIndexes.contains(absolutePath))
    {
      QStandardItem *item = new QStandardItem();
      item->setData(absolutePath, PathRole);
```

```
        appendRow(item);
    }
  }
}
```

Let's take this method by method:

- The constructor creates an instance of `QFileSystemWatcher`, which monitors the paths you give for changes to files or directories in the background, emitting the `directoryChanged` and `fileChanged` signals for the directories or files that change, respectively. We'll initialize this watcher with the desired path in the `setPath` method.

- The `roleNames` method establishes the relationship between the name of our data role, path, and the enumeration value we use to fetch this data from the model. As noted before, Qt expects this relationship in a hash table of role enumerations and their textual names. Qt Quick will use the values in the hash to determine the appropriate roles to fetch data, so I can simply refer to the field path in my QML, and under the hood, the Qt Quick engine fetches the value from the corresponding role value.

- The `setRootPath` method must first reset the model's contents, and then if the watcher was watching a directory, stop watching the old directory before watching the directory you pass. Once the code initializes the watcher, it forces a model update by invoking the same slot that the watcher invokes (remember the `connect` instance in the constructor?) whenever the directory changes.

- The `onDirectoryChanged` slot gets a list of PNG and JPEG files in the directory it's passed; then, it synchronizes the model by first deleting anything in the model that's not on the disk and then adding anything that's on the disk to the model. As we walk the model for the first time to process any deletes, we build a hash table of the files in the model; later, when we go to add items to the model, we can just check the hash table for entries. This is a little faster than a sequential search of the model or a list of the model's contents, because a hash table search is usually faster than a sequential search.

Summary

In this chapter, you took a whirlwind tour of Qt Quick, Qt's declarative framework for application development. You learned about the basic visible items that Qt Quick provides as a foundation for application development as well as Qt Quick's support for animations and transitions. Finally, you saw how to link Qt Quick and C++, giving you the best of both worlds in Qt development.

In the next chapter, we will take a look at Qt Quick's support for multimedia recording and playback. Stay tuned!

8
Multimedia and Qt Quick

Today's applications increasingly use multimedia to enhance their appeal to users. Sound effects are a key part of most user interfaces, and many applications include video tutorials or other video content. Some applications even use the camera provided on many devices; this is especially true of mobile applications, where most mobile devices have at least one, if not two, or more cameras.

In this chapter, we will take a look at Qt Quick's support for multimedia. We'll begin with an overview of what's possible so that you understand what you can and can't build using the platform-agnostic support for multimedia that Qt provides. Next, we will look at the Qt Quick components that provide access for audio and video playback in detail as well as how to use the camera, if it is supported.

In this chapter, we will cover the following topics:

- Multimedia in Qt
- Audio clips and sound effects
- Video clips
- Camera access

Multimedia in Qt

Qt has long provided some support for multimedia on the platforms it supports in C++ through the inclusion of its Phonon library. In Qt 5.0 and beyond, Qt Quick provides several objects to interact with the native support Qt and the underlying platform provides. Using these QML components, you can:

- Play sound clips and short sound effects in the background
- Play video content
- Display the camera viewfinder
- Capture camera content from the camera

What's actually supported by Qt depends on the target platform; for example, if the hardware doesn't have a camera, you can't display a camera viewfinder or take pictures. In practice, the level of support varies further; for example, as I write this, multimedia and support on Windows is very poor. Moreover, the actual format of the audio and video which Qt can play back depends on the libraries installed with Qt, which depend on the target platform. Platforms such as Linux might require additional libraries to fully support the audiovisual coder/decoders (codecs) used by many audio and video files.

To use any of the multimedia types we will discuss in this chapter, your QML must import the QtMultimedia module, as follows:

```
import QtMultimedia 5.0
```

 In this chapter, we'll focus on the Qt Quick multimedia interfaces. If you're interested in using the lower-level C++ APIs, see the Qt Multimedia documentation at http://qt-project.org/doc/qt-5/ multimediaoverview.html.

Playing audio clips and sound effects

Qt Quick provides the SoundEffect type to play short sound effects with a minimum latency. This is especially good for things such as button click sounds, virtual keyboard sounds, and alert tones as part of a rich and engaging multimedia experience. Using it is straightforward; you provide the type with a source field and call its play method to start the playback, as follows:

```
import QtQuick 2.3
import QtMultimedia 5.0

Text {
    text: "Click Me!";
    font.pointSize: 24;
    width: 150; height: 50;

    SoundEffect {
        id: playSound
        source: "soundeffect.wav"
    }
    MouseArea {
        id: playArea
        anchors.fill: parent
        onPressed: { playSound.play() }
    }
}
```

Here, SoundEffect will play the contents of the soundeffect.wav file stored in the application's resource when you click on the mouse area. You can stop a sound effect by calling its stop method, or else it simply plays until it gets completed.

The SoundEffect type has some additional fields that change how the sound effect is played:

- The loops field indicates the number of times the sound should be looped in the playback once you invoke play

- The loopsRemaining field indicates how many loops of playback remain while the sound is playing

- The playing field is true while the sound is playing

- The volume field indicates the volume, which spans from 0.0 (no audio) to 1.0 (the loudest possible volume)

- The status field is an enumeration that indicates the state of playback. It can be one of the following:

    ◦ SoundEffect.Null: no sound has been set

    ◦ SoundEffect.Loading: the sound is being loaded

    ◦ SoundEffect.Ready: the sound is ready to be played

    ◦ SoundEffect.Error: an error occurred during loading or playback

For longer bits of audio, it's best to use the Audio type. The Audio type's use is similar; you give it a source indicating where the audio should come from and then invoke its play method to start the playback. You can pause the playback by invoking its pause method, stop the playback by invoking its stop method, or seek a time offset in the audio by invoking seek and passing an offset in the time to seek (assuming that the audio source supports seeking; some sources such as web streams do not). You can use one as follows:

```
import QtQuick 2.3
import QtMultimedia 5.0

Text {
    text: "Click Me!";
    font.pointSize: 24;
    width: 150; height: 50;

    Audio {
        id: playMusic
        source: "music.wav"
    }
```

```
    MouseArea {
        id: playArea
        anchors.fill: parent
        onPressed:  { playMusic.play() }
    }
}
```

The `Audio` type includes the following properties that affect the playback:

- `autoLoad`: This defaults to true and forces the element to start loading the media on initialization

- `autoPlay`: This defaults to false, but when it is true, it starts the playback once the element has loaded on initialization

- `bufferProgress`: This is a real number in the range of 0.0 to 1.0, indicating how full the playback buffer is

- `duration`: This indicates the duration of the audio clip

- `error` and `errorString`: These contain error information in the event of a playback failure

- `hasAudio` and `hasVideo`: These indicate whether or not the clip has audio and video, respectively

- `loops`: This indicates the number of times that the audio should be played

- `muted`: This is true if the audio has been muted by the user

- `position`: This indicates the position in the playback of the audio

- `seekable`: This property is true if the audio stream supports seeking

- `volume`: This indicates the playback volume as a real number from 0.0 (no audio) to 1.0 (full volume)

The `Audio` type also has a `metaData` property that includes information about the audio being played, if it is encoded in the stream. It includes fields such as `albumArtist`, `albumTitle`, `audioBitRate`, `category`, `comment`, `composer`, `conductor`, `copyright`, `coverArtUrlLarge`, `coverArtUrlSmall`, `date`, `description`, `director`, `genre`, `language`, `lyrics`, `mood`, `posterUrl`, `publisher`, `sampleRate`, `size`, `subTitle`, `title`, `trackCount`, `trackNumber`, `writer`, and `year`.

Similar to the `Audio` type is the `MediaPlayer` type, which supports the playback of both audio and (as we'll see in the next section) video playback. For audio playback, its use is identical to the `Audio` type.

Playing video clips

Playing video is as easy as playing audio; there's a `Video` type that supports playing the video and displaying the video on the display. Here's a video player that plays video when you click on it and pauses and restarts the playback when you press the Space bar:

```
import QtQuick 2.3
import QtMultimedia 5.0

Video {
    id: video
    width : 800
    height : 600
    source: "video.avi"

    MouseArea {
        anchors.fill: parent
        onClicked: {
            video.play()
        }
    }

    focus: true
    Keys.onSpacePressed:
        video.playbackState == MediaPlayer.PlayingState ?
            video.pause() :
            video.play()
}
```

The `Keys` type emits signals for the various keys that are pressed; here, we're tying the `spacePressed` signal to a script that pauses and plays a video.

Most of the properties of `Video` are the same as of `Audio`, except that there's no `metaData` property. It's a subclass of `Item`, so the usual positioning properties such as `anchors`, x, y, `width`, and `height` are available to place the item in its parent. Note that all the transforms might not be available on the `Video` instances for performance reasons; for example, you usually can't freely rotate one.

You can also play the video content with a MediaPlayer instance and a VideoOutput instance. The VideoOutput type is also a subclass of Item like Video, and is essentially a rendering canvas for the video codec associated with a MediaPlayer instance to render the video. You use it by specifying a MediaPlayer instance in its source property, as follows:

```
import QtQuick 2.3
import QtMultimedia 5.0

Rectangle {
    width: 800
    height: 600
    color: "black"

    MediaPlayer {
        id: player
        source: "file://video.webm"
        autoPlay: true
    }

    VideoOutput {
        id: videoOutput
        source: player
        anchors.fill: parent
    }
}
```

Here, the MediaPlayer instance will play video.webm as soon as it's loaded, and the video will appear in the VideoOutput item, which is sized to fill the parent rectangle. Generally, you'll want to just use the Video instance, unless you need to have multiple playback windows, or else display a camera viewfinder, which we'll discuss next.

Due to the nature of the video codecs, although VideoOutput is a subclass of Item, not all transformations are supported; for example, you can't rotate the video player, nor can you place items on top of it and expect it to draw the child objects. This makes sense, when you think of the many codecs today that run directly on the graphics hardware of the host system.

VideoOutput has only a few properties. These are:

- autoOrientation: This, when true, uses the screen orientation to orient the video.

- contentRect: This indicates the content rectangle in the VideoOutput item where the video should be rendered.

- `fillMode`: This can be one of `Stretch`, `PreserveToFit`, or `PreserveAspectCrop`, indicating whether the video should be stretched, have its aspect ratio preserved, or the aspect ratio is preserved by cropping the image when rendering to the content rectangle. (The default is to preserve the aspect ratio and to fit the video in the rectangle.)

- `orientation`: This lets you set the orientation of the video at increments of 90 degrees. This is most useful when using the `VideoOutput` class as a camera viewfinder, which we'll discuss in the next section.

- `sourceRect`: This specifies the source rectangle from which the video should be considered for rendering.

Accessing the camera

To access the camera when it is supported by the hardware and Qt Multimedia, use the `Camera` type and its associated types to control the camera's capture behavior, exposure, flash, focus, and image processing settings. A simple use of the camera to show a viewfinder looks like the following code:

```
import QtQuick 2.3
import QtMultimedia 5.0

Item {
    width: 640
    height: 480

    Camera {
        id: camera
    }

    VideoOutput {
        source: camera
        anchors.fill: parent
    }
}
```

In short, the `Camera` type acts like a source for the video just as a `MediaPlayer` instance does.

The `Camera` type provides a few properties to control its behavior. They are:

- `imageCapture`: This is an instance of `CameraCapture`, which defines how the camera should capture an image

- `videoRecording`: This is an instance of `CameraRecorder`, which defines how the camera should capture a video

- **exposure**: This is an instance of `CameraExposure`, which controls the various options for the exposure mode of the camera
- **focus**: This is an instance of `CameraFocus`, which controls the auto- and manual-focusing behaviors
- **flash**: This is an instance of `CameraFlash`, which controls the camera flash
- **imageProcessing**: This is an instance of `CameraImageProcessing`, which controls the real-time image processing pipeline options such as white balance, saturation, and sharpening

The types associated with these fields can't be instantiated directly.

To have the camera take a picture, specify the `imageCapture` property and invoke its capture method, as follows:

```
import QtQuick 2.3
import QtMultimedia 5.0

Item {
    width: 640
    height: 360

    Camera {
        id: camera

        imageCapture {
            onImageCaptured: {
                // Show the preview in an Image
                photoPreview.source = preview
            }
        }
    }

    VideoOutput {
        source: camera
        focus : visible // to receive focus and capture key events
          when visible
        width: 320
    height: 180
    anchors.top: parent.top
    anchors.horizontalCenter: parent.horizontalCenter
```

```
        MouseArea {
            anchors.fill: parent;
            onClicked: camera.imageCapture.capture();
        }
    }

    Image {
        id: photoPreview
        width: 320
        height: 180
        anchors.bottom: parent.bottom
        anchors.horizontalCenter: parent.horizontalCenter
    }
}
```

Here, the camera displays its viewfinder in the top `VideoOutput` item and has an `Image` item at the bottom to display the captured image. When you touch the viewfinder, the QML invokes the `capture` method of `imageCapture`, which is part of `Camera`, capturing the image and updating the bottom image.

The `imageCapture` property of the `Camera` item also has a `capturedImagePath` property, which is a string to the path where the last captured image is stored.

Recording works in a similar manner; you specify the attributes of the recording, such as the desired codec in the `videoRecording` property, and then invoke its `record` and `stop` methods to start and stop recording. The resulting video will be stored at the location indicated by the property's `actualLocation` field.

 For more information on the actual attributes available to applications using the `Camera` type, see the Qt Multimedia documentation for the `Camera` type at `http://qt-project.org/doc/qt-5/cameraoverview.html`.

Summary

In this chapter, you saw the types that Qt Quick provides for managing audio and video media as well as how to control the camera if one exists. Using these types, you can add sound effects and an ambient audio to your applications as well as play video from resources, the filesystem, or the Web. In addition, you can control the camera, if one exists, and capture still and moving images with it.

In the next chapter, we will look at the support that Qt has for accessing hardware sensors, such as those pertaining to the device location, orientation, and power state.

9
Sensors and Qt Quick

Many of today's devices come with a myriad of sensors, including a means to determine the device's position and orientation as well as measure the characteristics of its surroundings through thermometers, luminescence sensors, accelerometers, gyroscopes, and other sensors. This is especially true of cell phones and other portable devices.

In this chapter, we will take a look at Qt's sensor and positioning frameworks as they're supported in QML. You'll learn how to determine a device's position on the surface of the earth and how to measure the other characteristics of its environment as reported by its onboard sensors.

In this chapter, we will cover the following topics:

- Sensors in Qt
- Determining the device location
- A simple example

Sensors in Qt

Qt has had a robust porting layer for device sensors for several years, starting with the Qt Mobility libraries meant to facilitate software development for cell phones. As Qt continued to evolve, support for sensors was added to Qt Quick, and the list of supported sensors grew. Today, Qt supports the following sensors:

- An accelerometer is supported through the `Accelerometer` type
- An altimeter is supported through the `Altimeter` type
- An ambient light sensor is supported through the `AmbientLightSensor` and `LightSensor` types

- An ambient temperature sensor is supported through the
  `AmbientTemperatureSensor` type
- A compass is supported through the `Compass` type
- A gyroscope is supported through the `Gyroscope` type
- Whether or not the device is in a holster is determined through the
  `Holster` type
- Proximity to the device's screen is determined through the
  `IRProximitySensor` and `ProximitySensor` types
- An ambient magnetic field is supported through the `Magnetometer` type
- The device's orientation is supported through the `OrientationSensor` type
- The rotation of the device is supported through the `RotationSensor` type
- How the device case is tapped on its *x*, *y*, and *z* axes is supported through
  the `TapSensor` type
- How the device is tilted is reported through the `TiltSensor` type

Each of these types has corresponding types that contain the reading; for
example, the `Accelerometer` type reports its current value through the
`AccelerometerReading` type.

To access the sensor library, you must add the `sensors` keyword to your `.pro` file,
as follows:

```
QT += qml quick sensors
```

The pattern to use all of these types is essentially the same: you import the
`QtSensors` module, instantiate a sensor, activate it or deactivate it, and connect a
script to its `readingChanged` slot. For example, to read from the accelerometer,
you'd write the following code:

```
import QtQuick 2.3
import QtQuick.Window 2.2
import QtSensors 5.0
Window {
    visible: true
    width: 360
    height: 360

    Accelerometer {
        id: accel
        dataRate: 100
        active: true
```

```
    onReadingChanged: {
        // the reading is in reading,
   // with x, y, and z properties
      }
   }
}
```

Sensors have three key properties that you need to know:

- `dataRate`: This indicates the rate at which the sensor should be sampled in milliseconds

- `active`: This indicates whether the application should sample the sensor (indicated by the value of `true`) or not

- `onReadingChanged`: This contains the script that processes the sensor reading, which is obtained by accessing the `reading` variable in the script you provide

Readings typically have properties for each of the readings; for example, three-dimensional readings have properties namely x, y, and z.

It's important to realize that although Qt has interfaces for all of these sensors, not every platform supports all of these sensors, and even on a particular platform (say, Android), different devices might have different sensors. For example, in Qt 5.3, Qt supports the accelerometer, ambient temperature sensor, gyroscope, light sensor, magnetometer, proximity sensor, and rotation sensor, but not other sensors. Moreover, not every Android device has these sensors; my Android tablet does not have a magnetometer. When designing your application, you need to take both these facts into account: which sensors are supported by the Qt porting layer for your target, and the kinds of sensors on the hardware that your target audience actually has. A matrix showing which platforms supported by Qt provide which sensors is available at `http://qt-project.org/doc/qt-5/compatmap.html`.

As I have discussed more in *Chapter 12, Developing Mobile Applications with Qt Creator*, sensors consume battery power, so your application should use them judiciously. Turn them on when you need to make a measurement by setting the active property, and turn them off when you're done.

Determining the device location

Many devices support position determination, either through hardware such as a **Global Positioning System (GPS)** receiver or through network resources such as **Internet Protocol (IP)** geolocation. Similar to the other sensor support, this facility was introduced to Qt in Qt 4.x through the Qt Mobility module and is now supported through the Qt Positioning module. It's supported on many mobile devices, including Android.

To use the Qt Positioning module, you need to include the positioning keyword in your `.pro` file, as follows:

```
QT += qml quick network positioning
```

The Qt Positioning module provides three types of positioning; you can access these by importing the `QtPositioning` module:

- `PositionSource`: This provides position updates at a specified rate, emitting the `positionChanged` signal when position updates are available
- `Position`: In the slot that you assign to the `positionChanged` signal, you'll receive a `Position` instance
- `Coordinate`: The `Position` instance has a `Coordinate` property that specifies the location of the device

The `PositionSource` type has the following properties:

- `active`: This, when true, indicates to the system that the positioning system should be activated and returns device positioning readings to your application
- `name`: This indicates the unique name of the positioning plugin that is currently reporting the device's position
- `preferredPositioningMethods`: This indicates your application's preferences for positioning. The preferred positioning methods can be one of the following:
    - `PositionSource.NoPositioningMethods`: This indicates that no positioning method is preferred
    - `PositionSource.SatellitePositioningMethods`: This indicates that satellite-based methods such as GPS should be preferred
    - `PositionSource.NonSatellitePositioningMethods`: This indicates that non-satellite-based methods such as IP geolocation should be preferred

- ○ PositionSource.AllPositioningMethods: This indicates that any positioning method is acceptable

- sourceError: This holds the error that last occurred with the PositionSource method

- supportedPositioningMethods: This indicates the supported positioning methods that are available

- updateInterval: This specifies the desired update interval in milliseconds

- valid: This specifies whether or not the positioning system has obtained a valid backend plugin to provide data

Here's a simple use of PositionSource:

```
PositionSource {
    id: src
    updateInterval: 1000
    active: true

    onPositionChanged: {
        var coord = src.position.coordinate;
        position.text =
                Math.abs(coord.latitude) +
                (coord.latitude < 0 ? " S " : " N " ) +
                Math.abs(coord.longitude) +
                (coord.longitude < 0 ? " W " : " E " );
    }
```

You can start positioning on PositionSource by calling its start method, or you can stop updating by calling its stop method. In addition to these, you can request for a one-shot positioning report by invoking its update method.

The Position type has a number of properties to encapsulate the device's position. These are:

- altitudeValid: This indicates whether the altitude reading is valid

- coordinate: This contains a coordinate with the latitude, longitude, and altitude

- directionValid: This indicates whether the direction is valid

- horizontalAccuracy: This indicates the degree of horizontal accuracy in the position reported

- horizontalAccuracyValid: This indicates whether the horizontal accuracy is valid

- `latitudeValid` and `longitudeValid`: This indicates whether the latitude and longitude are valid

- `speed`: This indicates the device's speed

- `speedValid`: This indicates whether the device's speed is valid

- `timestamp`: This indicates when the measurement was taken

- `verticalAccuracy`: This indicates the vertical accuracy of the measurement

- `verticalAccuracyValid`: This indicates whether the vertical accuracy is valid

- `verticalSpeed`: This indicates the vertical speed of the device

- `verticalSpeedValid`: This indicates whether the vertical speed is valid

All distances and speeds are in metrics, and the latitude and longitude are in decimal degrees, using the WGS-84 datum.

In addition to providing the latitude, longitude, and altitude of the device, the `Coordinate` type offers the `distanceTo` and `azimuthTo` methods, letting you compute the distance between two `Coordinate` instances or the bearing from one `Coordinate` instance to another. It also provides the `atDistanceAndAzimuth` method, computing the destination point when you travel a particular distance at a specific azimuth from the coordinate's latitude and longitude. These methods are the solutions to the so-called *forward geodetic problem* and *reverse geodetic problem*, very much used in cartography. Go to `http://www.ngs.noaa.gov/TOOLS/Inv_Fwd/Inv_Fwd.html` for details on how these are computed.

The following code shows how a simple use of the `PositionSource` type might look:

```
import QtQuick 2.3
import QtQuick.Window 2.2
import QtPositioning 5.2

Window {
    visible: true
    width: 360
    height: 360

    Text {
        id: positionLabel
        text: qsTr("Position:")
        anchors.top: parent.top
        anchors.left: parent.left
    }
```

```
Text {
    id: position
    text: qsTr("Hello World")
    anchors.horizontalCenter: parent.horizontalCenter
    anchors.top: parent.top
}

PositionSource {
    id: src
    updateInterval: 1000
    active: true

    onPositionChanged: {
        var coord = src.position.coordinate;
        position.text =
                Math.abs(coord.latitude) +
                (coord.latitude < 0 ? " S " : " N " ) +
                Math.abs(coord.longitude) +
                (coord.longitude < 0 ? " W " : " E " );
    }
}
}
```

Here, the `PositionSource` type is active on application start and updates once per second. When it receives a position report, it emits a `positionChanged` signal, which triggers the `onPositionChanged` script. This obtains the coordinate from the position and formats it for presentation in the `position` text field.

Like other device sensors, obtaining position reports uses additional battery power over normal program execution. Generally, your application should only determine the device's position when it actually needs it, such as before submitting the position to a service in order to determine nearby points of interest or to tag the user's location in some way. In general, you should not run the positioning system all the time (unless you're building an application that needs it, such as a turn-by-turn navigation application), because doing so can greatly diminish battery life.

Obtaining a device's position – a simple example

Let's close this chapter with a simple example that returns the device's position, accelerometer, gyroscope, ambient light, and magnetometer readings. Here's how our application looks when running on a Nexus 7:

Note that my Nexus 7 does not have a magnetometer, so these readings aren't being updated.

First, we need to ensure that we include the positioning and sensor modules in our .pro file (if we don't, the application will compile but fail to launch):

```
TEMPLATE = app

QT += qml quick positioning sensors

SOURCES += main.cpp

RESOURCES += qml.qrc
# Additional import path used to resolve QML modules in Qt
  Creator's code model
QML_IMPORT_PATH =

# Default rules for deployment.
include(deployment.pri)
```

Next, we move on to the QML itself. This is long, but straightforward:

```qml
import QtQuick 2.3
import QtQuick.Window 2.2
import QtPositioning 5.2
import QtSensors 5.0

Window {
    visible: true
    width: 360
    height: 360

    Text {
        id: positionLabel
        text: qsTr("Position:")
        anchors.top: parent.top
        anchors.left: parent.left
        color: position.valid ? "red" : "black"
    }

    Text {
        id: position
        text: qsTr("Hello World")
        anchors.horizontalCenter: parent.horizontalCenter
        anchors.top: parent.top
    }

    PositionSource {
        id: src
        updateInterval: 1000
        active: true

        onPositionChanged: {
            var coord = src.position.coordinate;
            position.text =
                    Math.abs(coord.latitude) +
                    (coord.latitude < 0 ? " S " : " N " ) +
                    Math.abs(coord.longitude) +
                    (coord.longitude < 0 ? " W " : " E " );
        }
    }

    LabelThreePart {
```

```
        id: accelerometerReading
        label: "Accel"
        anchors.top: position.bottom
        anchors.horizontalCenter: parent.horizontalCenter
    }

    Accelerometer {
        id: accel
        dataRate: 100
        active:true

        onReadingChanged: {
            accelerometerReading.xValue = reading.x
            accelerometerReading.yValue = reading.y
            accelerometerReading.zValue = reading.z
        }
    }

    LabelThreePart {
        id: gyroscopeReading
        label: "Gyro"
        anchors.top: accelerometerReading.bottom
        anchors.horizontalCenter: parent.horizontalCenter
    }

    Gyroscope {
        id: gyroscope
        dataRate: 100
        active: true

        onReadingChanged: {
            gyroscopeReading.xValue = reading.x
            gyroscopeReading.yValue = reading.y
            gyroscopeReading.zValue = reading.z
        }
    }

    Text {
        id: lightSensorLabel
        anchors.top: gyroscopeReading.bottom
        anchors.right: lightSensorValue.left
        text: qsTr("Light Sensor:")
```

```
    }

    Text {
        id: lightSensorValue
        anchors.top: lightSensorLabel.top
        anchors.horizontalCenter: parent.horizontalCenter
        text: "N/A"
    }

    // Light Sensor
    LightSensor {
        id: lightSensor
        dataRate: 100
        active: true

        onReadingChanged: {
            lightSensorValue.text = reading.illuminance
        }
    }

    // Magnetometer
    LabelThreePart {
        id: magnetometerReading
        label: "Mag"
        anchors.top: lightSensorValue.bottom
        anchors.horizontalCenter: parent.horizontalCenter
    }

    Text {
        id: magcLabel
        anchors.right: magcValue.left
        anchors.top: magnetometerReading.bottom
        text: "Mag Cal: "
    }
    Text {
        id: magcValue
        anchors.horizontalCenter: parent.horizontalCenter
        anchors.top: magcLabel.top
        text: "N/A"
    }

    Magnetometer {
```

```
            onReadingChanged: {
                magnetometerReading.xValue = reading.x
                magnetometerReading.yValue = reading.y
                magnetometerReading.zValue = reading.z
                magcValue.text = reading.calibrationLevel
            }
        }
    }
}
```

First up is the position label and position field, which we color red if `PositionSource` is unable to get a fix. The remainder of the sensors come next, using a little `LabelThreePart` control that I wrote, which looks as follows:

```
import QtQuick 2.3

Rectangle {
    property string label: "Something"
    property alias xValue: xValue.text
    property alias yValue: yValue.text
    property alias zValue: zValue.text


    width: parent.width
    height: 32

    Text {
        id: xLabel
        anchors.left: parent.left
        anchors.top: parent.top
        text: label + " X: "
    }
    Text {
        id: xValue
        anchors.left: xLabel.right
        anchors.top: parent.top
        text: "N/A"
    }

    Text {
        id: yLabel
        anchors.right: yValue.left
        anchors.top: parent.top
        text: label + " Y: "
```

```
    }

    Text {
        id: yValue
        anchors.horizontalCenter: parent.horizontalCenter
        anchors.top: parent.top
        text: "N/A"
    }

    Text {
        id: zLabel
        anchors.right: zValue.left
        anchors.top: parent.top
        text: label + " Z: "
    }

    Text {
        id: zValue
        anchors.right: parent.right
        anchors.top: parent.top
        text: "N/A"
    }
}
```

This is just a rectangle containing six fields; it uses its `label` property to create meaningful labels for the x, y, and z values to be shown, along with property aliases to the text fields which actually show those values.

Summary

In this chapter, you learned how to determine measurements from device sensors including the device's positioning system, accelerometer, and other sensors. In the next chapter, we will take a look at how we can use Qt's localization framework and tools to localize your application.

10
Localizing Your Application with Qt Linguist

Localization is an important yet commonly neglected part of software development today. Most authors of applications, irrespective of whether those applications are commercial or open source, hope to capture a large number of users for their applications. Increasingly, this means supporting multiple languages in multiple locales, often needing support for multiple languages in one locale (think of it as French and English coexisting in Canada).

Since a long time, Qt has had a framework for making applications easy to localize with tools that help you to avoid hardcoding strings in your application and a GUI named **Qt Linguist** to help manage translation. In this chapter, we will take a look at Qt's strategy for localization, discussing the three tools (lupdate, lrelease, and Qt Linguist) that Qt provides and how to use them, along with what you need to do as you write your application to take advantage of Qt's localization framework.

In this chapter, we will take a look at the following topics:

- Understanding the task of localization
- Marking strings for localization
- Localizing your application with QLinguist
- Including localized strings in your application
- Localizing special parameters—currencies and dates with QLocale

Understanding the task of localization

Localizing your application has several phases that typically overlap throughout a project's life cycle. These phases are:

1. As you write your application, you place strings to localize in your application in a specific way so that Qt can identify the strings as needing localization.

2. Periodically, you extract all the strings in your application and give them to translators in order to translate.

3. Translators provide translations for the strings in your application.

4. You compile translation files with the translated strings for each language you want to support.

5. The `tr` and `qsTr` functions for C++ and QML let you identify the strings in your application that require localization. Qt provides four tools to facilitate these phases.

6. The `lupdate` command generates a list of the strings that need localization in your application.

7. Translators use Qt Linguist to provide translations of the strings in your application.

8. The `lrelease` command takes the translated strings from Qt Creator and packages them in a format for your application to consume.

The following figure shows how these phases interact:

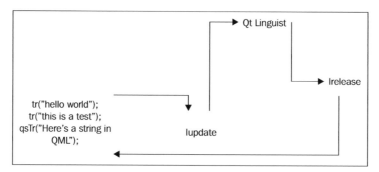

Software development is iterative, and localization is no exception. Small projects might prefer to do the localization just once, or perhaps twice, waiting until the application is nearly done before submitting the application strings for localization. Larger applications, or larger companies with a dedicated staff of translators, might prefer a more iterative approach, going through the localization cycle several times throughout application development. Qt supports both models.

Marking strings for localization

All the way back in *Chapter 1*, *Getting Started with Qt Creator*, I told you to always mark your strings for localization using the `tr` and `qsTr` functions: `tr` for C++ and `qsTr` for QML strings. Doing so has two key advantages:

- First, it enables Qt to find every string that needs localization
- Second, if you install a Qt translator object in your application and provide a translation file, the strings you wrap with these functions are automatically replaced by their localized equivalent

Let's examine the use of `tr` in more detail. All Qt objects that include the `Q_OBJECT` macro in their declaration include the `tr` function. You've seen it with one argument, as follows:

```
button = new QPushButton(tr("&Quit"), this);
```

The leading `&` in the string isn't for the `tr` function, but it is for the keyboard accelerators; you can prefix a letter with `&` to assign a keyboard accelerator and it gets the default system (a key combination with *Alt* for Windows, *Command* for Apple, and *Alt* for Linux). The `tr` function uses the string you pass as the string in the user interface if no translated version of the string appears in the application's current translation table, or it uses the string in the current translation table if one exists.

The `tr` function can take a second argument, a disambiguation context that `tr` uses for the same string that might require different translations:

```
tr("&Copy", "Menu");
```

This function can also handle strings with plurals, as follows:

```
tr("%n item(s) replaced", "", count);
```

Depending on the value of count and the locale, a different string is returned. So, a native English translation could return `"0 items replaced"`, `"1 item replaced"`, `"2 items replaced"`, and so on, while a French translation could return `"0 item remplacé"`, `"1 item remplacé"`, `"2 items remplacés"`, and so on.

The `qsTr` function in QML works similarly but does not have the flexibility that the `tr` method has for disambiguation or handling plurals.

Localizing your application with QLinguist

Once you've marked your strings using `tr` or `qsTr`, you need to generate a table of those strings for Qt Linguist to localize. You can do this using the `lupdate` command, which takes your `.pro` file and walks your sources to look for strings to localize and creates an XML file of the strings you need to translate for Qt Linguist. You need to do this once for each language you want to support. When doing this, it's best to name the resulting files systematically; one way to do this is to use the name of the project file, followed by a dash, followed by the ISO-639-2 language code for the language.

A concrete example is in order. This chapter makes use of `QtLinguistExample`; we can run `lupdate` using a command such as this to create a list of strings that we'll translate to Esperanto (ISO-639-2 language code EPO):

```
% lupdate -pro .\QtLinguistExample.pro -ts .\QtLinguistExample-epo.ts
```

Don't forget that the `%` character is the command prompt, which might differ from system to system.

Here, the `-pro` file indicates the `.pro` file that contains the list of sources to scan for strings to translate, and the `-ts` argument indicates the name of the translation file to be written. You'll need `lupdate` in your path, of course. How you set your path will depend on whether you're working on Windows, Mac OS X, or Linux, and where you've installed Qt. Some installations of Qt might update your path automatically, while others might not do so. On my Windows machine, for example, I can find `lupdate` at `C:\qt\5.1.0\msvc2012_64\bin\lupdate.exe`.

The `.ts` file is an XML file with tags to indicate the strings to be translated, their context in your application's source code, and so forth. Qt Linguist will save the translations to its output file, which is named with a QM suffix as well, but don't worry: `lupdate` is smart enough to not overwrite the existing translations if you run it again after providing some translations.

Qt Linguist is a GUI application; on starting this application, you'll see a screen very similar to the next screenshot:

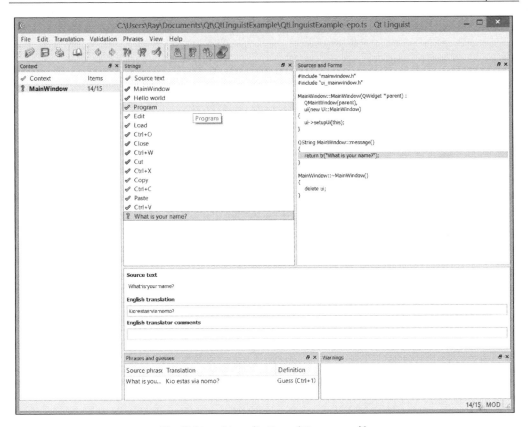

The Qt Linguist application editing a `.qm` file

To begin, you need to open a `.ts` file you generated, by navigating to **File | Open**, and choosing a translation file. You'll be prompted for the destination language, and then you're given a list of the strings found. You—or your translators—only need to walk through each string and enter the corresponding string in the translated language. As you do so, you can see the context of the string in the source code in the right-most pane; the line of the source from which the string was captured is highlighted.

Qt Linguist lets you track which strings you've translated and also those which still need translation. The icon to the left-hand side of each of the strings can be one of the following:

- A black question mark, indicating that a string is yet to be translated

- A yellow question mark, indicating that the string doesn't pass all of Qt Linguist's validation tests, but you're ignoring the failures

- An exclamation point, indicating that the string you've provided doesn't pass Qt Linguist's validation tests

- A yellow checkbox, indicating that you've provided a translation, but Qt Creator might have found a problem with it

- A green checkbox, indicating that the string has been translated and is ready to go

Qt Linguist provides some simple validation tests, such as ensuring that strings with `printf`-style arguments have the same number of arguments in each translation.

Qt Linguist also supports phrase books; you might be able to download a phrase book with common strings already localized to the language you're targeting.

At any point, you can generate a translation file for inclusion in your application by running `lrelease`. For example, to create one for our Esperanto strings, we'd use `lrelease` as follows:

```
% lrelease .\QtLinguistExample-epo.ts .\QtLinguistExample-epo.qm
```

This takes the incoming `.ts` file and generates a `.qm` file with the strings. The `.qm` files are highly compressed binary files used by Qt directly in the process of rendering the application.

Including localized strings in your application

In order to supply translated strings to the `tr` and `qsTr` functions in your application, your application needs to include a `QTranslator` object to read the `.qm` files and replace the strings provided to `tr` and `qsTr` with their translated counterparts. We can do this in your main entry point function, as follows:

```
QApplication a(argc, argv);
QTranslator translator;
bool result = translator.load("QtLinguistExample-epo.qm");
a.installTranslator(&translator);

    // Other window setup stuff goes here

return a.exec();
```

This code allocates a `QTranslator` object and loads the indicated translation file into the translator before installing it into the `QApplication` object. In this example, we're hardcoding the language in order to localize to Esperanto.

Note that if you want to support the locale as picked by the system, you might choose to do it this way:

```
QString locale = QLocale::system().name();
QTranslator translator;
translator.load(QString("QtLinguistExample-") + locale);
```

The QLocale class here is a class for managing the system's locale. Here, we use it to determine the system's locale, and then we attempt to load the localized string file for the system's current locale.

For this to work, the .qm files for the application need to be locatable by the application. They should be in the output directory; one way to do this during development is to turn off shadow builds in Qt Creator, under **Build Settings** in **Project Pane**. As you build your application's installer—a platform-specific task outside the scope of this book—you need to include your .qm files with the application binary.

> For more information on Qt Linguist, see its manual at http://qt-project.org/doc/qt-5/qtlinguist-index.html.

Localizing special parameters – currencies and dates with QLocale

A common thing you might need to do is localize currencies and dates. Qt makes this easy, although the solution isn't obvious until you've thought about it a bit.

First, you need to know about the QString arg method. It replaces an escaped number with the formatted version of its argument; if we write:

```
QString s = QString("%1 %2").arg("a").arg("b");
```

Then, s contains the string "a b". Second, you need to know about the toString method of QLocale which formats its argument in a locale-specific way.

So, we could write:

```
QString currencyValue = QString("%1 %2")
    .arg(tr("$")).arg(QLocale::toString(value, 'g', 2)
```

This uses tr to localize the currency symbol and the QLocale class's static method, toString, to convert the value of the currency to a string with the locale-specific decimal separator (a period in the US and Canada, and a comma in Europe).

Date formatting is similar; the `toString` method of `QLocale` has overloads for the `QDateTime`, `QDate`, and `QTime` arguments, so you can simply write:

```
QDateTime whenDateTime = QDateTime::currentDateTime();
QString when = QLocale::toString(whenDate);
```

This gets the current date and time and stores it in `whenDateTime` and then makes a string out of it using the locale's default formatting. The `toString` method can take a second argument that determines the output format; it's one of the following:

- `QLocale::LongFormat`: This uses the long version of month and day names
- `QLocale::ShortFormat`: This uses the short version of day and month names
- `QLocale::NarrowFormat`: This provides the narrowest form of formatting for the date and time

Summary

Localizing applications with Qt is easy with Qt Linguist and the localization framework in Qt. To use the framework, though, you must mark your strings to localize with `tr` or `qsTr` in your source code wherever they appear. Once you do this, you can create a source file of strings to translate with QLinguist using Qt's `lupdate` command and then provide translations for each string. Once you've provided the translations, you compile them using `lrelease`, and then include them in your application by installing a `QTranslator` object in your application's main function and by loading the translation table generated by `lrelease`.

In the next chapter, we will take a look at another important aspect of software development that Qt Creator supports: performance analysis with the QML Profiler and Valgrind.

11
Optimizing Performance with Qt Creator

We don't use performance analysis tools every day, but we're glad that they're there when we need them. Commercial tools such as the ones that come with Microsoft Visual Studio or standalone tools such as IBM's Rational Rose Purify can set you back a pretty pile of change—fortunately, Qt Creator has most of what you need built-in or has support for working with open source tools to help you profile the runtime and the memory performance of your application.

In this chapter, we will see how to perform the runtime profiling of QML applications using the QML performance analyzer and learn how to read the reports it generates. We will then turn our attention to memory performance analysis with Valgrind using Qt Creator, which is a free option that helps you look for memory leaks and heap corruption on the Linux platform.

In this chapter, we will take a look at the following topics:

- The QML performance analyzer
- Finding memory leaks with Valgrind

The QML performance analyzer

Qt Quick applications are supposed to be fast, with smooth and fluid user interfaces. In many cases, this is easy to accomplish with QML; the contributors to QML and the Qt Quick runtime have put a great deal of effort into creating an environment that performs well under a wide variety of circumstances. Sometimes, however, try as you might, you might find that you just can't squeeze the performance out of your application that you'd like. Some mistakes are obvious, such as the following:

- Doing a lot of compute-intensive tasks between state changes or actions that trigger drawing operations

- Excessively complex view hierarchies with thousands of elements on display at once

- Running on very limited hardware (often in combination with the first two problems)

Knuth famously said, "Premature optimization is the root of all evil," and he's definitely right. However, there might come a time when you will need to measure the performance of your application, and Qt Creator includes a special performance analyzer for just this purpose. With this, you can see how much time your application spends in each QML method as well as measure the critical aspects of your application which are at the edge of your control, such as how long it takes to create your application's view hierarchy.

Let's take a closer look.

QtSlowButton – a Qt Quick application in need of performance tuning

Let's analyze the performance of QtSlowButton, a poorly performing example program that I have put together for you for this chapter. The QtSlowButton program has two QML components: a button based on the calculator button from *Chapter 3, Designing Your Application with Qt Designer*, and a view with buttons that you can press. Here's the button implementation:

```
import QtQuick 2.2

Rectangle {
    id: button

    width: 128
    height: 64

    property alias label: buttonText.text
```

```
property int delay: 0

color: "green"

Rectangle {
    id: shade
    anchors.fill: button;
    color: "black"; opacity: 0
}

Text {
    id: buttonText
    anchors.centerIn: parent;
    color: "white"
    font.pointSize: 16
}

MouseArea {
    id: mouseArea
    anchors.fill: parent
    onClicked: {
        for(var i = 0; i < button.delay; i++);
    }
}

states: [
    State {
        name: "pressed"; when: mouseArea.pressed == true
        PropertyChanges { target: shade; opacity: .4 }
    }
]
}
```

Each button simply runs a `for` loop when you press it; its `delay` property controls the number of cycles through the loop. In addition, each button has a `label`, which the button draws in the center of the clickable area.

The main user interface consists of three buttons in a `Column`, labeled `"fast,"` `"medium,"` and `"slow,"` with progressively longer delays:

```
import QtQuick 2.2

Rectangle {
    width: 180
    height: 360

    Column
    {
        spacing: 20
```

```
Button
{
    delay: 10000;
    label: "fast";
}
Button
{
    delay: 100000;
    label: "medium";
}
Button
{
    delay: 300000;
    label: "slow";
}
    }
}
```

You can either load the source project that comes with this book for this example, or you can create a new Qt Quick project and build a `Button` and a main view with this code.

Perform the following steps to analyze the application's performance:

1. Build the application.

2. Select **QML Profiler** from the **Analyze** window. The application will start, and Qt Creator will switch to the **Analyze** view.

3. Click on each button for a few times. Expect to wait after you click on a button.

4. Quit the application.

> The QML Profiler uses TCP/IP to make a connection between the running application and the profiler, by default, on port 3768. You might have to tinker with your host's firewall settings in order to get things to work correctly. On Windows, be sure to permit the connection in the Windows Firewall dialog that appears.

The following figure shows the **Analyze** view after the application is run. The **QML Profiler** has the following three tabs and shows the first tab by default:

- The first tab is **Timeline**, indicating what happened at which point of time through the application and how long it took
- The second tab, **Events**, lists the events that the QML application processed and how much time was spent on each event
- The third tab, **JavaScript**, lists the JavaScript functions that the program encountered while running and the time that the application spent in the total running of each function

In the following screenshot, I've clicked on the **Handling Signal** row to expand the signals that the application handled. You can see that it handled one signal, the `onClicked` signal, for a total of three times and the amount of time spent each time is shown as varying bars on the graph. Clearly, if this were doing real work, there'd be an opportunity for performance improvement here.

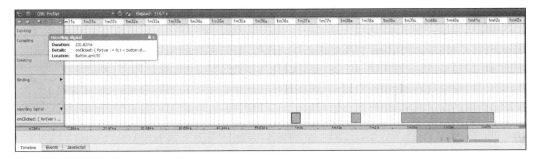

The next screenshot shows a different view of this information, the JavaScript run time for your application. This indicates that up to the limit of numerical accuracy, the application spent all of its measured time on the `onClicked` handler for the button—clearly, a performance *hot spot* in this case. Interestingly, every incident of my JavaScript is measured here, including the `$when` clause that puts the opaque filter in front of the button when it's pressed. Looking at this view can be very helpful if you need to look at where things are happening in your application in a broad sense.

Location	Time in Perce	Total Time	Self Time in F	Self Time	Details
Button.qml:30	100.56 %	9.830 s	99.84 %	9.760 s	onClicked
<program>	100.00 %	9.775 s	0.00 %	0.000 µs	Main Program
Button.qml:37	0.14 %	13.727 ms	0.14 %	13.727 ms	$when
Button.qml:37	0.02 %	1.961 ms	0.02 %	1.961 ms	(anonymous function)

Caller	Total Time	Caller Description		Callee	Total Time	Callee Description
<program>	9.770 s	Main Program		Button.qml:30	60.790 ms	onClicked
Button.qml:30	60.790 ms	onClicked		Button.qml:37	7.844 ms	$when
				Button.qml:37	1.961 ms	(anonymous function)

Timeline Events JavaScript

The next screenshot is likely to be most interesting to performance geeks, because it shows the amount of time QML spent for each and every event it handled while running the application. Again, we can see that the `onClicked` handler consumes a lion's share of the processor resources, but other things such as the creation of the rectangles for the view and the variable binding for the state of a push button are shown as well. Typically, we'll use the **JavaScript** view to get a broad picture of where the problems in your application are located, while we'll use the **Events** view to zero in on specific problems.

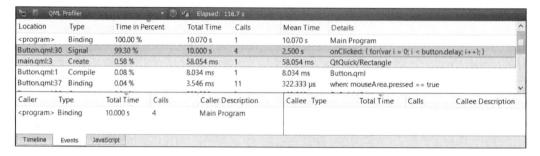

Finding memory leaks with Valgrind

As discussed in *Chapter 3*, *Designing Your Application with Qt Designer*, you should really get in the habit of using Qt's parent-child relationship when managing the memory for the classes based on `QObject` in your application to avoid memory leaks. In my time of writing Qt applications, the only time I've had to deal with memory leaks was when I didn't use memory management based on `QObject`. In addition, using classes such as `QSharedPointer` for pointers that aren't based on `QObject` is a good idea too.

Sometimes, though, you might introduce a memory leak that you can't find on your own. In that case, a tool such as Valgrind can be a lifesaver; it tracks every memory allocation and free operation in your application, alerting you when your program terminates if it hasn't freed all the memory it allocates.

Unfortunately, Valgrind is supported by Mac OS X and Linux-only. If you're writing pure Qt code, this shouldn't be a serious issue for you even if you're developing on Windows or Mac OS X, because you can port your application to Linux and run it in Valgrind there. To do this, you'll want to use an application such as VMware Fusion, VMware Player, Microsoft Hyper-V, or Parallels to set up a virtual machine running Linux (I like to use Ubuntu), install Qt Creator, and get your code running there. Unfortunately, if you have Windows-specific code or libraries in your application, this isn't an option. If you build your application for Windows, a commercial leak detector such as Rational Rose Purify might be an option.

Before continuing, you should make sure that you have Qt Creator running under a Linux distribution, and install Valgrind from `http://bit.ly/14QwiQZ` or use your Package Manager. For example, on Ubuntu, I can install Valgrind with the following command:

```
sudo apt-get install valgrind
```

When you use Valgrind, you actually run your application inside Valgrind; instead of starting your application, you start Valgrind, which starts your application.

In the next section, we will see a complete example.

QtLeakyButton – a Qt C++ application in need of memory help

QtLeakyButton is an application that does one thing: presents a button that when clicked, allocates 512 KB of RAM. Here's the code (you can either run the sample code that accompanies this book, or create a Qt GUI application with a single button and a label and use this code for your `MainWindow` class):

```cpp
// mainwindow.h
#ifndef MAINWINDOW_H
#define MAINWINDOW_H

#include <QMainWindow>

namespace Ui {
    class MainWindow;
}

class MainWindow : public QMainWindow
```

```
{
    Q_OBJECT

public:
    explicit MainWindow(QWidget *parent = 0);
    ~MainWindow();

public slots:
    void leakPressed();

private:
    Ui::MainWindow *ui;
    int m_count;
};

#endif // MAINWINDOW_H

// mainwindow.cpp

#include "mainwindow.h"
#include "ui_mainwindow.h"

MainWindow::MainWindow(QWidget *parent) :
    QMainWindow(parent),
    ui(new Ui::MainWindow),
    m_count(0)
{
    ui->setupUi(this);
    connect(ui->leakButton, SIGNAL(clicked()),
            this, SLOT(leakPressed()));
}

MainWindow::~MainWindow()
{
    delete ui;
}

void MainWindow::leakPressed()
{
    void *p = new char[512 * 1024];
    m_count++;
    ui->leakCount->setText(QString::number(m_count));
}
```

The MainWindow class has an integer counter and an ui slot for the instantiated form. The MainWindow constructor instantiates this form and then connects the leakButton clicked signal to MainWindow::leakPressed. The leakPressed method just allocates memory and bumps the counter, updating the counter with the number of times you've pressed the button.

To use Valgrind, we need to add a new run target to your application. To accomplish this, perform the following steps:

1. Click on **Projects** on the left-hand side and then click on **Run**.
2. Click on **Add** under the header and select the **Custom Executable** option.
3. For **Name**, enter `valgrind`.
4. For `Executable`, add the path to `valgrind` (usually, `/usr/bin/valgrind`).
5. For arguments, (replace `<your-app-target-name>` with your application's name as you specify it in the .pro file) enter:

   ```
   -q --tool=memcheck --leak-check=full --leak-resolution=low
   ./<your-app-target-name>
   ```

   Make sure you are running the file in the same directory as your build—the binary.

6. For **Working Directory**, enter `$BUILDDIR`.

Now, you can select the Valgrind run target for your application. You need to do this with the debug build, because Valgrind needs the debug symbols in your application to produce a meaningful report. To use Valgrind, start the application and click on the button a few times. The Valgrind process outputs information continually, but most of the output comes after we quit the application.

Valgrind produces a lot of output, which can take you some time to sort through. We're looking for the leak summary, which indicates the number of bytes that are definitely lost and indirectly lost. Definitely lost blocks are the memory you've allocated and not freed; indirectly lost memory is the memory that has leaked because it's referred to by another pointer and the referring pointer wasn't freed. The output will look something similar to the following code:

```
X bytes in 1 blocks are definitely lost in loss record n of m
    at 0x........: function_name (filename:line number)
```

The `X` indicates the number of bytes that leaked, and the address of the leaked block is shown in the second line. The record numbers indicate the internal record numbers used by the application's memory allocator and probably won't help you much.

We should focus on leaks in our application, because it's possible that Qt might have leaks of its own. Valgrind supports suppression files that indicate which leaks should be ignored; if you can find and download one for the version of Qt you're building against, you can include a reference to the suppression file by modifying the argument line to read as follows:

```
-q --tool=memcheck --leak-check=full --leak-resolution=low
--suppressions=suppression.txt ./[your-app-target-name]
```

Finding memory leaks in your application is partly art and partly science. It's a good exercise to go through periodically during application development in order to ensure that the leaks you might introduce are quickly found while you're most familiar with the new code you're running.

Summary

Qt Creator provides the QML analyzer, which lets you perform a runtime analysis of your Qt applications. You can see a graph (in time) of how your application is running, as well as dive into the details about how your application spends its time drawing, binding to variables, and executing JavaScript.

Qt Creator also integrates well with Valgrind on Linux, letting you look for memory leaks in your application. Using Valgrind on Linux, you can see the blocks that were allocated but not freed, and more importantly, see how big they were and where they were allocated in the code, giving you a head start in determining why they were not freed.

In the next chapter, we will turn our attention from specific parts of Qt Creator to one of its most exciting aspects in general: the ability to use Qt Creator to compile and test applications for mobile platforms such as Google Android.

12
Developing Mobile Applications with Qt Creator

Qt and mobile development have a long history. Qt's beginnings included early releases on Linux personal digital assistants in the late Nineties and at the turn of this century. Since then, it's been ported to a number of mobile environments, including the mobile variants of Linux that Nokia shipped such as MeeGo and Symbian. While Symbian and MeeGo came and went, Qt's acceptance of mobile platforms lives on, most recently with support for Android.

In this chapter, we will talk a little about writing mobile applications and then learn how to set up Qt Creator to write applications for Android. It's worth noting that while we will leverage everything you have learned about Qt development when developing a mobile application, we also need to understand how the environments that the mobile software runs on are different from traditional desktop and laptop environments as well as how to design those constraints. Once we understand these differences, writing software for mobile platforms such as Android with Qt is a matter of snapping your fingers!

We will cover the following topics in this chapter:

- A mobile software development primer
- Setting up Qt Creator for Android
- Supporting other mobile platforms

A mobile software development primer

The key point to remember when developing software for any mobile platform, such as a cell phone or tablet, is that every resource is at a premium. The device is smaller, meaning:

- Your user will pay less attention to your application and use it for shorter periods of time

- The screen is smaller, so you can display less information on the display (don't be fooled by the high dot pitch of today's displays; reading a six-point font on a four-inch display is no fun, high pixel densities or not.)

- The processor and graphics processing unit are slower

- There's less RAM and less graphics memory

- There's less persistent storage for your application's data

- The network is slower, by as much as three orders of magnitude

Let's take a look at each of these in more detail.

User attention is at a premium

Can you walk and chew gum at the same time? I can't, but many people walk, chew gum, and use their mobile devices at the same time (worse, some even drive while using their devices). It's very rare for an application on a cell phone or tablet to have 100 percent of the user's attention for more than a few minutes at a time. A good rule of thumb is the smaller the device, the more likely is the user bound to treat it as something to pick up and glance at, or use while they're doing something else.

The limited attention that your user gives to your application has three key consequences:

- Your application must be fast. Mobile devices are no place for extra progress bars, spinning cursors, or lengthy splash screens.

- Your application must be succinct. The best mobile applications show data only on a page or two, having very flat navigation hierarchies. A common structure is to have a single screen with information and a single screen with preferences that lets you configure what information should be shown (such as, the location for which you're getting the information). Favor clear iconography over verbose text—if you can't draw, find someone who can, or buy icons from a site such as The Noun Project (http://thenounproject.com/).

- Your application must be accessible. Buttons should be big (a good guideline is that no hit target in your application should be smaller than the pad of your finger, which is about a square centimeter), and text should be bigger, if possible.

For these reasons, Qt Quick is a better choice for most mobile applications that you'll write. You can create smooth, responsive applications that are visually pleasing and don't overwhelm your users.

Computational resources are at a premium

Mobile devices must carry their power source with them: batteries. While batteries have improved over the last 20 years, they haven't kept up with Moore's Law; most of the improvements have been made on the processor side, as processors have become smaller and dissipate less heat in the course of a normal operation.

Nonetheless, mobile devices aren't as fast as desktops or laptops—a good way to think about it is that the last generation's processor design probably scales well for mobile devices today. That's not to say that mobile devices are slow, but just that they're slower. An equally important point to consider is that you can't run the processor or graphics processor at full tilt without seriously affecting the battery life.

Qt—especially Qt Quick—is optimized for low power consumption, but still there are things that you can do to help squeeze the best performance out of your mobile application:

- **Don't poll**: This is probably the single most important point. Use Qt's asynchronous signal-slot mechanism wherever possible, and consider multithreading using QThread and the rest of Qt's multithreading environment, if you need to do something in the background. The more your application sleeps, the more it prolongs the battery life.

- **Avoid gratuitous animations**: Some amount of animation is both customary and important in today's applications; well-thought-out animations can help orient the user as to where they've come from in an application's user interface and where they're going. However, don't flash, blink, or otherwise animate just to see pixels move; under the hood, a lot has to take place to move those pixels, and this consumes battery.

- **Use the network judiciously**: Most mobile devices have at least two radios (cellular and Wi-Fi); some have more. Accessing the network should be seen as a necessary evil, because radios consume power when transmitting and receiving data. Also, don't forget data parsing: if you're parsing a lot of data, it's likely that you're running the CPU at full tilt to do the heavy lifting and that means a lower battery life.

Network resources are at a premium

You've already been warned about the high cost to the battery for using the network. To add insult to injury, most mobile devices run on networks that can be up to three orders of magnitude slower than a desktop; your office desktop might have a gigabit Ethernet, but in many parts of the world, a megabit a second is considered fast. This situation is rapidly improving as network operators deploy cellular wireless networks such as **Long Term Evolution** (**LTE**) and Wi-Fi hotspots everywhere, but these are by no means uniformly available. On a recent trip in California, in the course of eight hours, my cellular network connectivity throughput ran a gamut from faster than my cable modem (running at 25 megabits a second) down to the dreaded megabit per second which can make a large web page crawl.

For most applications, you should be fine with the **Hyper Text Transfer Protocol** (**HTTP**); Qt's QNetworkAccessManager class implements HTTP and HTTPS, and using HTTP means that you can build web services to support your backend in a standard way.

If you're developing a game or a custom application, you might need to build a custom protocol. Consider using QTcpSocket or QUdpSocket for your network protocol, keeping in mind of course that TCP is a reliable protocol. However, with UDP, there's no guarantee of your data reaching its destination; reliability is up to you.

Something to make a special note of is error handling in networked applications; unlike a desktop, where network failures are likely to be rare because your computer is tethered to the network, wireless networks can suffer all sorts of transitory problems. These don't necessarily lead to logical failures; a short drop in network connectivity can result in Domain Name Service problems, Transport Layer Security timeouts, or retry timeouts. Handle errors in your application, and ensure that there are mechanisms to retry important network operations, such as data synchronization and content uploads. Be prepared for duplicate requests and uploads too, in the cases where your device uploads something to a server which doesn't get an acknowledgement from the server because of a network problem and tries again.

Storage resources are at a premium

Mobile devices typically use all the solid-state memory. Although solid-state memory has come down in price significantly in the last several years, it's still not as cheap as the rotating magnetic memory that makes up the disk drives in most desktops and many laptops. As a result, mobile devices might have as little as 8 GB of flash memory for persistent storage, or if you're lucky, 16 or 32 GB. This is shared across the system and all the applications; your application shouldn't use more than a few gigabytes at most, and that's only if your user is expecting it, say for a podcast application. That should be the sum total of the size of your application: its static resources such as audio and video, and anything it might download and cache from the network.

An equally important point is that the runtime size of your application needs to be smaller. Most mobile devices have between a half-gigabyte and 2 GB of dynamic RAM available; the system shares this across all running applications, so it's important to allocate only what you need and free it when you're done.

Finally, don't forget that your graphics textures and things can eat valuable GPU memory as well. While Qt manages the GPU for you, whether you're using Qt or Qt Quick, you can write an application that consumes all of the device's texture memory, making it difficult or impossible for the native OS to render what it needs, if it needs to interrupt your application with another application or system message.

To port or not to port?

To paraphrase the immortal bard, that's the question. With Qt's incredible flexibility across numerous platforms, the temptation to grab an existing application and port it can be overwhelming, especially in the vertical markets where you have a piece of custom software written in Qt for the desktop and you have a customer who wants *the same thing* for the latest mobile device for their mobile workers. In general, the best advice I can offer you is to avoid porting UI and to only port the business logic in an application if it seems well-behaved for mobile devices.

UI ported from the desktop or a laptop environment seldom works well on mobile devices. The user's operating patterns are just too different: what a person wants to do while seated at a desktop or laptop is just not the same as what they want to—or can—do when they are standing up, walking around, or in brief spurts in a conference room, cafeteria, or café. If you're porting from one mobile device to another, it might not be so bad; for example, a developer with a Qt application for MeeGo, Nokia's Linux-based platform, shouldn't have too much problem bringing their application to Qt on Android, BlackBerry, or iOS.

Porting business logic might be a safer bet, assuming that it doesn't make heavy use of the CPU, network, or dynamic or static storage. Qt offers a wrapper for SQLite through QtSql, and many enterprise applications use that for local storage. This is a reasonable alternative for data storage, and most HTTP-based networking applications shouldn't be too hard on the network layer, as long as they have reasonable caching policies and don't make too many requests for data too often. However, if the application uses a lot of storage or has a persistent network connection, it's time to rearchitect and rewrite.

A word on testing

Testing any application is important, but mobile applications require an additional effort in testing, especially Android applications. There's a wide variety of devices in the market, and users expect your application to perform well on any device they might have.

The most important thing you can do is test your application on real devices—as many of them as you can get your hands on—if you're interested in releasing your application commercially. While the Android SDK used by Qt Creator comes with an emulator that can run your Android application on your desktop or laptop, running on an emulator is no substitute for running on the device. A lot of things are different, from the size of the hardware itself to having a touchscreen, and of course, the network connection and raw processing power.

Fortunately, Android devices aren't terribly expensive, and there are an awful lot of them around. If you're just starting out, eBay or the Google Play Store can be a good place to shop for an inexpensive used or new device. If you're a student or a budding entrepreneur, don't forget that many family members might have an Android device that you can borrow; or, you can use the Android cell phone that you already have.

When and what should you test? Often, and everything! In a multi-week project, you should never be more than a few days away from a build running on a device. The longer you spend in writing the code that you haven't tested on a device, the more assumptions you will make about how the device will perform, with most of those assumptions turning out wrong.

Be sure to not just test your application in good circumstances but in bad ones as well. Network connectivity is a prime example; you should test the error handling in cases with no network coverage. If you have a good network coverage where you're working, one trick you can use is to put the device in a metal cookie tin or paint can; the metal attenuates the signal and has the same effect as the signal being lost in the real world (say, in a tunnel or in the subway).

Setting up Qt Creator for Android

Android's functionality is delimited in API levels; Qt for Android supports Android level 10 and above: that's Android 2.3.3, a variant of Gingerbread. Fortunately, most devices in the market today are at least Gingerbread, making Qt for Android a viable development platform for millions of devices.

Downloading all the pieces

To get started with Qt Creator for Android, you're going to need to download a lot of stuff. Let's get started:

1. Begin with a release of Qt for Android, which was either. If it was not part of the Qt installation you downloaded in *Chapter 1, Getting Started with Qt Creator*, you need to go back and download it from `http://qt-project.org/downloads`.

2. The Android developer tools require the current version of the **Java Development Kit (JDK)** (not just the runtime, the Java Runtime Environment, but the whole kit and caboodle); you can download it from `http://www.oracle.com/technetwork/java/javase/downloads/jdk7-downloads-1880260.html`.

3. You need the latest Android **Software Development Kit (SDK)**, which you can download for Mac OS X, Linux, or Windows at `http://developer.android.com/sdk/index.html`.

4. You need the latest Android **Native Development Kit (NDK)**, which you can download at `http://developer.android.com/tools/sdk/ndk/index.html`.

5. You need the current version of Ant, the Java build tool, which you can download at `http://ant.apache.org/bindownload.cgi`.

Download, unzip, and install each of these, in the given order. On Windows, I installed the Android SDK and NDK by unzipping them to the root of my hard drive and installed the JDK at the default location I was offered.

Setting environment variables

Once you install the JDK, you need to be sure that you've set your JAVA_HOME environment variable to point to the directory where it was installed. How you will do this differs from platform to platform; on a Mac OS X or Linux box, you'd edit .bashrc, .tcshrc, or the likes; on Windows, go to **System Properties**, click on **Environment Variables**, and add the JAVA_HOME variable. The path should point to the base of the JDK directory; for me, it was C:\Program Files\Java\ jdk1.7.0_25\, although the path for you will depend on where you installed the JDK and which version you installed. (Make sure you set the path with the trailing directory separator; the Android SDK is pretty fussy about that sort of thing.)

Next, you need to update your PATH to point to all the stuff you just installed. Again, this is an environment variable and you'll need to add the following:

- The bin directory of your JDK
- The android\sdk\tools directory
- The android\sdk\platform-tools directory

For me, on my Windows 8 computer, my PATH includes this now:

```
...C:\Program Files\Java\jdk1.7.0_25\bin;C:\adt-bundle-
windows-x86_64-20130729\sdk\tools;;C:\adt-bundle-
windows-x86_64-20130729\sdk\platform-tools;...
```

Don't forget the separators: on Windows, it's a semicolon (;), while on Mac OS X and Linux, it's a colon (:).

> An environment variable is a variable maintained by your operating system which affects its configuration; see http://en.wikipedia.org/wiki/Environment_ variable for more details.

At this point, it's a good idea to restart your computer (if you're running Windows) or log out and log in again (on Linux or Mac OS X) to make sure that all these settings take effect. If you're on a Mac OS X or Linux box, you might be able to start a new terminal and have the same effect (or reload your shell configuration file) instead, but I like the idea of restarting at this point to ensure that the next time I start everything up, it'll work correctly.

Finishing the Android SDK installation

Now, we need to use the Android SDK tools to ensure that you have a full version of the SDK for at least one Android API level installed. We'll need to start Eclipse, the Android SDK's development environment, and run the Android SDK manager. To do this, follow these steps:

1. Find Eclipse. It's probably in the Eclipse directory of the directory where you installed the Android SDK. If Eclipse doesn't start, check your JAVA_HOME and PATH variables; the odds are that Eclipse will not find the Java environment it needs to run.

2. Click on **OK** when Eclipse prompts you for a workspace. This doesn't matter; you won't use Eclipse except to download Android SDK components.

3. Click on the **Android SDK Manager** button in the Eclipse toolbar (circled in the next screenshot):

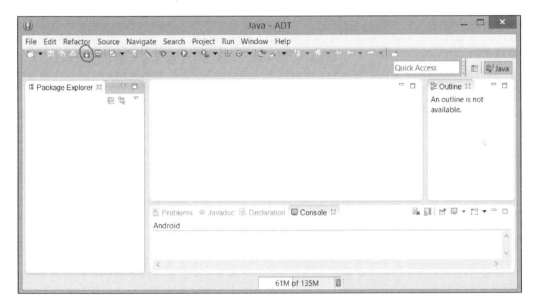

4. Make sure that you have at least one Android API level above API level 10 installed, along with the Google USB Driver (you'll need this to debug on the hardware).

5. Quit Eclipse.

Next, let's see whether the Android Debug Bridge—the software component that transfers your executables to your Android device and supports on-device debugging—is working as it should. Fire up a shell prompt and type adb. If you see a lot of output and no errors, the bridge is correctly installed. If not, go back and check your PATH variable to be sure it's correct.

While you're at it, you should developer-enable your Android device too so that it'll work with ADB. Follow the steps provided at http://bit.ly/1a29sal.

Configuring Qt Creator

Now, it's time to tell Qt Creator about all the stuff you just installed. Perform the following steps:

1. Start Qt Creator but don't create a new project.
2. Under the **Tools** menu, select **Options** and then click on **Android**.
3. Fill in the blanks, as shown in the next screenshot. They should be:
    ° The path to the SDK directory, in the directory where you installed the Android SDK.
    ° The path to where you installed the Android NDK.
    ° Check **Automatically create kits for Android tool chains**.
    ° The path to Ant; here, enter either the path to the Ant executable itself on Mac OS X and Linux platforms or the path to ant.bat in the bin directory of the directory where you unpacked Ant.
    ° The directory where you installed the JDK (this might be automatically picked up from your JAVA_HOME directory), as shown in the following screenshot:

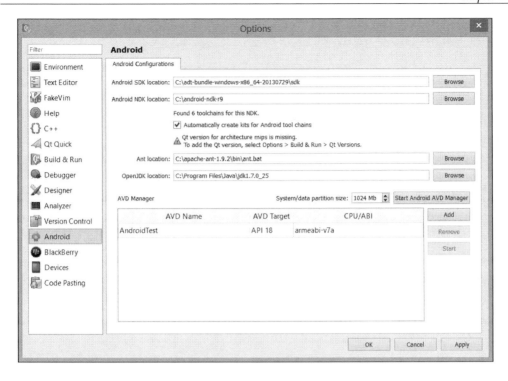

4. Click on **OK** to close the **Options** window.

You should now be able to create a new Qt GUI or Qt Quick application for Android! Do so, and ensure that Android is a target option in the wizard, as the next screenshot shows; be sure to choose at least one ARM target, one x86 target, and one target for your desktop environment:

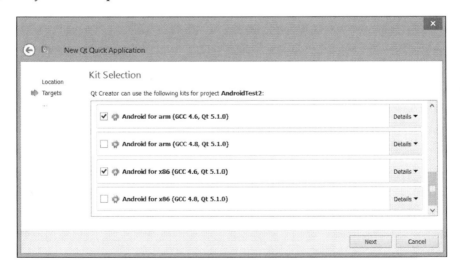

If you want to add Android build configurations to an existing project, the process is slightly different. Perform the following steps:

1. Load the project as you normally would.
2. Click on **Projects** in the left-hand side pane. The **Projects** pane will open.
3. Click on **Add Kit** and choose the desired Android (or other) device build kit.

The following screenshot shows you where the **Projects** and **Add Kit** buttons are in Qt Creator:

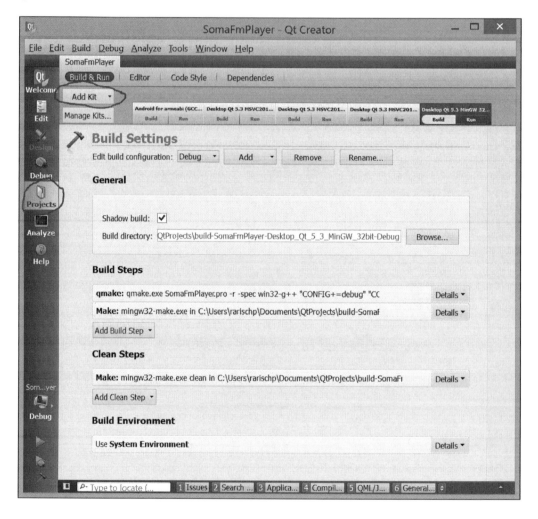

Building and running your application

Write and build your application normally. A good idea is to build the Qt Quick Hello World application for Android first before you go to town and make a lot of changes, and test the environment by compiling for the device. When you're ready to run on the device, perform the following steps:

1. Navigate to **Projects** (on the left-hand side) and then select the **Android for arm** kit's **Run Settings**.

2. Under **Package Configurations**, ensure that the Android SDK level is set to the SDK level of the SDK you installed.

3. Ensure that the **Package name** reads something similar to `org.qtproject.example`, followed by your project name.

4. Connect your Android device to your computer using the USB cable.

5. Select the **Android for arm** run target and then click on either **Debug** or **Run** to debug or run your application on the device.

Supporting other mobile platforms

In addition to supporting Android, Qt supports iOS and BlackBerry; other platforms might be supported in the future. For more information on Qt's support for mobile platforms, see the Qt documentation at `http://qt-project.org/doc/qt-5/mobiledevelopment.html`.

Summary

Qt for Android gives you an excellent leg up on mobile development, but it's not a panacea. If you're planning to target mobile devices, you should be sure to have a good understanding of the usage patterns for your application's users as well as the constraints in CPU, GPU, memory, and network that a mobile application must run on.

Once we understand these, however, all of our skills with Qt Creator and Qt carry over to the mobile arena. To develop for Android, begin by installing the JDK, Android SDK, Android NDK, and Ant, and then develop applications as usual: compiling for the device and running on the device frequently to iron out any unexpected problems along the way.

In our final chapter, we will learn about the bunch of odds and ends in Qt Creator and Qt in general, which will make software development much easier.

13
Qt Tips and Tricks

In the previous chapters, we discussed what makes Qt great for software development: how to edit, compile, and debug applications; how to profile their execution and memory performance; how to localize them for different regions of the world; as well as how to make mobile applications that run on Android phones and tablets. In this chapter, we will discuss a collection of tips and tricks that you should know about when using Qt Creator and Qt, which will have you writing software like a pro.

We will cover the following topics in this chapter:

- Writing console applications with Qt Creator
- Integration with version control systems
- Configuring the coding style and coding format options
- Building projects from the command line
- Setting the Qt Quick window display options
- Learning more about Qt
- Debugging Qt's signal-slot connections

Writing console applications with Qt Creator

Remember Hello World in *Chapter 1, Getting Started with Qt Creator*? That was a console application, about as simple a one as you can write. Let's recap the code; we created a new Qt console application, and in `main.cpp`, wrote the following lines of code:

```
#include <QCoreApplication>
#include <iostream>
```

```
using namespace std;

int main(int argc, char *argv[])
{
    QCoreApplication a(argc, argv);

    cout << "Hello world!";

    return a.exec();
}
```

Any valid C++ file is valid in a Qt application, including **Standard Template Library (STL)** code. This is especially handy if you need to write a small tool in C++ and haven't learned a lot about Qt yet—everything you know about C++ (and even C, if you prefer) is accessible to you in Qt Creator.

Although Qt is most widely known as a GUI toolkit, it's worth mentioning that the QtCore library, a part of every Qt application including Qt console applications, includes a bevy of utility and template classes, including the following:

- Collection classes, including QList, QVector, QStack, and QQueue to keep lists and vectors and for the last-in-first-out and first-in-first-out data storages

- Dictionary classes (otherwise known as hash tables), including QMap and QHash

- A cross-platform file's I/O with QFile and QDir

- Unicode string support with QString

Why will you choose Qt's classes over what straight C++ provides you? There are a few reasons:

- **Memory performance**: Unlike STL collections, Qt collections are reference-based and use copy-on-write to save memory. Qt collections typically consume less memory than their STL counterparts.

- **Iteration**: Iterating over Qt collections is safe, with a guarded access to prevent you from walking off the end of a collection.

- **Readability**: Using Qt code and libraries throughout an application provides a uniform look and feel that can make the code easier to maintain.

- **Portability**: On some embedded platforms where Qt is available, STL might not be present. However, this isn't nearly the problem that it was when Qt was first being written.

It's worth noting that Qt's collections are often slightly slower than their STL counterparts: when using a Qt class for data, you're often trading memory performance for speed. In practice, however, this is rarely a problem.

The `QFile` and `QDir` classes deserve a special mention because of one thing: portability. Even directory separators are handled in a portable way; directories are always demarcated by a single /, regardless of whether you're running on Mac OS X, Linux, or Windows, which makes it easy to write the code in a platform-agnostic way and to ensure that it runs on all the platforms. Under the hood, Qt translates directory strings to use the platform-specific directory separator when accessing files.

Integrating Qt Creator with version control systems

Nearly all large projects require some sort of version control to coordinate the changes made to the same files by different users and to ensure that changes to a source base occur harmoniously. Even a single developer can benefit by using version control, because version control provides a record of what has changed in each file that the developer has edited and provides a valuable history of the project over time. Qt Creator supports the following version control systems:

- Bazaar (supported in Qt Creator Version 2.2 and beyond)
- CVS
- Git
- Mercurial (supported in Qt Creator version 2.0 and beyond)
- Perforce (supporting Perforce Server version 2006.1 and later)
- Subversion

The first thing you need to do is set up version control software for your project. How to do this depends on the version control system you choose (it might be dictated by your organization, for example, or you might have a personal preference from working on past projects), and how you do this differs from system to system. So, we won't go into it here. However, you need to have a repository to store the versions of your source code and have the appropriate version control software installed on your workstation with the appropriate directories containing the version control binaries in your system's PATH variable so that Qt Creator can find them. It's important that you are able to access the version control commands from your system's shell (such as PowerShell or your local terminal prompt), because Qt Creator accesses them in the same way.

Once you've done this, you can configure how Qt Creator interacts with version control by navigating to **Tools | Options | Version Control**. The following screenshot shows this window:

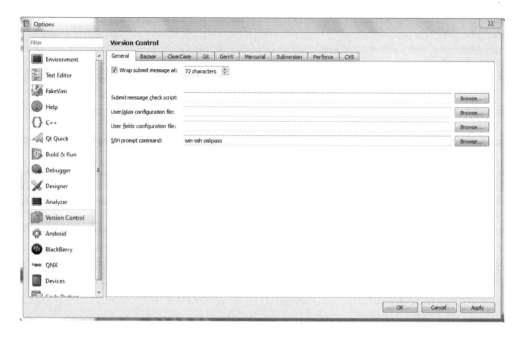

There are general configuration options, which apply to any version control system you're using, and then there are specific options for each flavor of version control that Qt supports. The following are the general options:

- A script that can be run on any submission message to ensure that your message is formatted correctly or contains the right information

- A list of names and aliases for your source code control system

- A list of fields to include in each submission message

- The SSH prompt command used to prompt you for your SSH password when using SSH in order to access your version control system

Some version control systems, such as Git and Mercurial, support local version control repositories. This comes in handy if you're flying solo on a development project and just need a place to back up your changes (of course, remember to back up the source code repository directory as well). If you're using one of these systems, you can use Qt to create the local repository directory directly by selecting **Create Repository** under **Tools**, or by going to **File | New File or Project** and then going to the last project management page. Of course, to do this, you'll need to have your version control software installed first.

You can find out more about how Qt Creator integrates with version control systems by taking a look at the Qt documentation at http://qt-project.org/doc/qtcreator-2.6/creator-version-control.html.

If you install and configure a version control system, the various commands available from this system are added in a submenu to the **Tools** menu of Qt Creator. From there, you can perform the following steps:

- View the version control command output by navigating to **Window | Output Panes | Version Control**.

- View diff output (a comparison between two files with the same name of different versions) from your version control system, letting you see what's changed in a file you are editing from what's in the repository.

- View the change log for a file under version control by selecting **Log** or **Filelog**.

- Commit a file's changes to the system by selecting **Commit** or **Submit**.

- Revert the changes to a file by selecting **Revert**. Update your working directory with the current contents of the version control system by clicking on **Update**.

- Use additional per-version-control commands to support branches, stashes, and remote repositories.

 If you're just starting out and need to choose a version control system, perhaps the best thing to do is to look at the comparison of various systems on Wikipedia, at http://en.wikipedia.org/wiki/Comparison_of_revision_control_software, and get familiar with one. Personally, I prefer Git for my work, using both local repositories and hosted repositories such as GitHub. It's free, fast, has a good support for branching, and is well-supported by Qt Creator.

Configuring the coding style and coding format options

Readable code is crucial, and Qt Creator's default coding style is one that most people find very readable. However, you might be on a project with different coding guidelines, or you might just find that you can't bear a particular facet of how the Qt Creator editor deals with code formatting; maybe it's the positioning of the brackets or how a switch statement gets formatted. Fortunately, Qt Creator is extremely configurable. Go to **Tools | Options | C++** and configure how Qt Creator will format your code, as shown in the following screenshot:

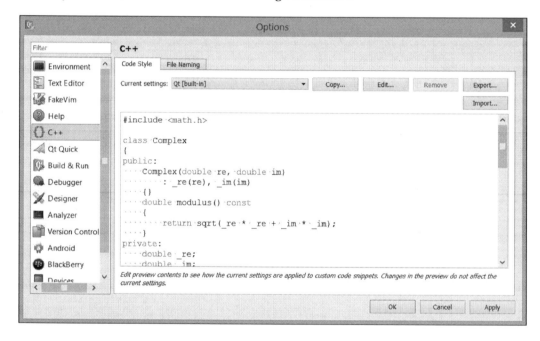

The basic dialog lets you pick popular formatting styles, such as Qt's default format or the format used by most GNU code. You can also click on **Edit**, which brings up the code style editor, which you can see in the next screenshot:

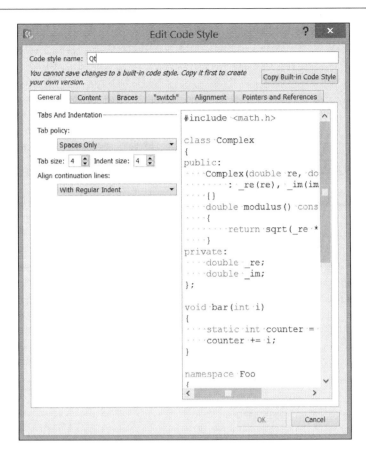

You'll want to begin by copying a built-in style and editing it to suit your tastes; from the **Edit Code Style** dialog, you can select whether tabs are spaces or tabs, the number of spaces per tab stop, as well as how line continuations are handled. Each pane lets you adjust specific aspects of code formatting:

- The **Content** pane lets you adjust how class bodies are formatted, including spacing for public, protected, and private declarations
- The **Braces** pane lets you control formatting that pertains to braces
- The **"switch"** pane lets you control the `switch` and `case` statement formatting
- The **Alignment** pane lets you control how code is aligned between consecutive lines
- The **Pointer** pane lets you control spacing around pointer declarations

It's easy to go crazy with all these options, but I urge you not to; what looks good at first glance is often an unreadable mess when you see it day after day. If you're just getting started with Qt, stick to the default formatting and remember the old adage "do no harm" when it comes to editing the existing code—match the formatting that's already there.

Building projects from the command line

Sometimes, you need to build a project from the command line. Maybe you're working on Linux and you're just more comfortable there, or you've got a remote session running on your desktop while you're in a meeting. Or, maybe you want to automate builds on a build server and need to know how Qt performs its compilation magic for your builds.

The trick lies in qmake: Qt's meta-make system that manages the generation of make files for the compiler toolchain you already have installed. The qmake command takes the .pro files, which you first saw in *Chapter 2, Building Applications with Qt Creator*, and generates the make or nmake file necessary for your tool chain to build your application.

First, ensure that you have your compiler and set utility in your system path; how you do this varies from one development environment to another. Next, be sure to have commands for Qt's build system in your path—a default if you've installed Qt on Linux using the package manager and easily done by editing your path to include the appropriate bin directory from the Qt tools you installed on Mac OS X or Windows.

Next, open up a command window and change to the directory containing your project: your .pro file should be at the root of this directory. Type qmake and then enter either make (if your build system uses make) or nmake (if you're using a Microsoft Windows tool chain). That's all there is to this!

If you have a C++ project, Qt or not, and you miss the .pro file, qmake can create this for you with the following command:

```
qmake -project
```

With this command, qmake explores all the C++ files in the folder and subfolders and writes a generic PRO file. Then, you can edit this file to change the target name or to add some qt modules as shown in the following statement, but in general, you will obtain a good result:

```
qt += qt network xml
```

Setting the Qt Quick window display options

Qt Quick is great for building applications for non-traditional computing environments, such as set-top boxes or automotive computers. Often, when working with Qt Quick, you'll want an application that doesn't have all the usual windows (such as the close box) around the contents of the window in these settings, because you're trying to present a unified user interface based on your Qt Quick application, rather than the windowing toolkit on the host platform.

You can easily set windows options by editing the main.cpp file in your Qt Quick project. By default, it looks similar to the following code snippet:

```
#include <QtGui/QGuiApplication>
#include "qtquick2applicationviewer.h"

int main(int argc, char *argv[])
{
    QGuiApplication app(argc, argv);

    QtQuick2ApplicationViewer viewer;
    viewer.setMainQmlFile(QStringLiteral(
        "qml/QtTranslucent/main.qml"));
    viewer.showExpanded();

    return app.exec();
}
```

This code creates a Qt Quick Application Viewer, sets its main QML file (the first file to be loaded) to the indicated file, and then shows it before starting the application's event loop. Fortunately, QtQuick2ApplicationViewer has a setFlags method that lets you pass the Qt::Window flags to the window it initializes in order to display your Qt Quick application. These flags include:

- Qt::FramelessWindowHint: This indicates that the window should be borderless (works on Linux systems but not on Windows).

- Qt::Popup: This indicates a popup window. You can use this on Windows to get a nearly borderless window with a slight drop shadow.

- Qt::WindowStaysOnTopHint: This indicates that the window should stay on top of all other windows.

- Qt::WindowStaysOnBottomHint: This indicates that the window should stay under all other windows.

- Qt::Desktop: This indicates that the window should run on the desktop.

A complete list of the flags can be found in the Qt documentation at `http://bit.ly/17NT0sm`.

You can also adjust a window's opacity using the `setOpacity` method of `QtQuick2ApplicationViewer`.

Say, for example, we want a blue window with no border but a slight drop shadow of 75 percent opacity to hover over all other windows of our Qt Quick application. We'd change the QML to read as follows:

```
import QtQuick 2.0

Rectangle {
    width: 360
    height: 360
    color: "blue"
    Text {
        text: qsTr("Hello World")
        anchors.centerIn: parent
        font.pointSize: 18
    }
    MouseArea {
        anchors.fill: parent
        onClicked: {
            Qt.quit();
        }
    }
}
```

Note the `color: blue` declaration for our top-level rectangle. Next, we will modify `main.cpp` to read as follows:

```
#include <QtGui/QGuiApplication>
#include "qtquick2applicationviewer.h"

int main(int argc, char *argv[])
{
    QGuiApplication app(argc, argv);

    QtQuick2ApplicationViewer viewer;
    viewer.setOpacity(0.75);
    viewer.setFlags(Qt::Popup | Qt::WindowStaysOnTopHint);
    viewer.setMainQmlFile(QStringLiteral(
        "qml/QtTranslucent/main.qml"));
```

```
    viewer.showExpanded();

    return app.exec();
}
```

The key lines here come just before `viewer.setMainQmlFile`: the `setOpacity` method sets the main window's opacity, and the `setFlags` method sets the flags for the main window to be a popup that will be on top of all other windows. On running the application, we will see something similar to the following screenshot:

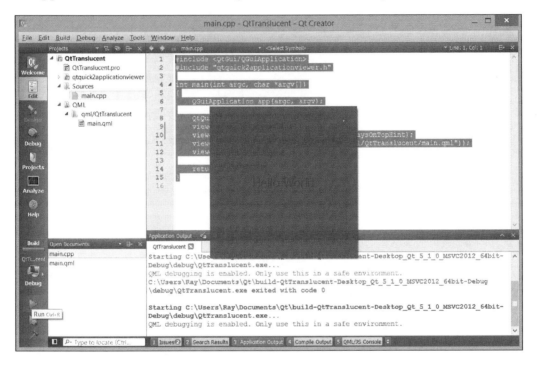

You can use this trick to come up with a variety of effects for how your Qt Quick application is displayed.

Learning more about Qt

In the first few chapters, I pointed you to the **Help** panel of Qt Creator as well as the editor's facility for the autocompletion of class members when editing code. Qt Creator's help view is really a subview of **Qt Assistant**, the full documentation for Qt. This should be installed by default if you install all of the Qt installation; the documentation is packaged as HTML files locally. Much of this documentation is also available on the Web, but it's much faster to access it this way.

When we start Qt Assistant from the Qt SDK (either from the command line with `qtassistant` or by finding it in the installed list of applications), we should see something similar to the following screenshot:

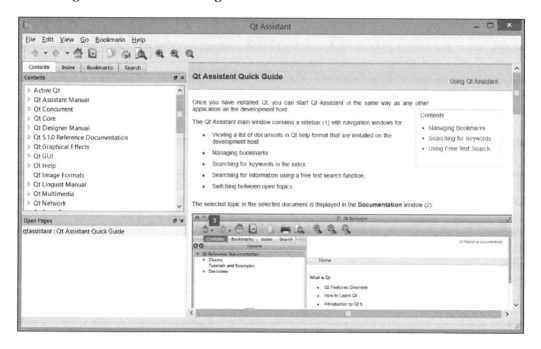

Qt Assistant is the definitive place to learn about Qt. In the column on the left-hand side, you can see a table of contents; the best place to start is with **Qt Core**, and then either **Qt GUI** or **Qt Quick**, depending on whether you want to write GUI or Qt Quick applications. The main view on the right-hand side is just like a browser window, complete with hyperlinks to the related sections.

Also, inside Qt Assistant, you can add bookmarks to frequently accessed pages, see an index of all the terms in the documentation, and quickly search for terms using the search tab in the column on the left-hand side. It's an invaluable resource and as easy to use as an e-book.

Finally, if you prefer to use the Web to learn about things, don't forget Qt's extensive on-line documentation, available at `http://qt-project.org/doc/`. There's also the Qt Project forums at `http://qt-project.org/forums`.

Debugging Qt's signal-slot connections

What do you do if you think that you've correctly connected a signal to a slot and yet your slot's not being fired?

Here's a bunch of things you can try:

- Check the compile log for error messages about undefined signals and slots.
- Check the runtime log for errors on connection. If need be, ensure that the connection succeeds by testing its return value (it should return true).
- Check to make sure that the `connect` code, the emit code, and the slot code is reached. (Odds are one of them isn't.)
- Make sure that you declare the connection as follows:

```
connect(sender, SIGNAL(someSignal(type)), receiver,
        SLOT(received(type)))
```

- The signal and slot specifications should have the argument types, but not the arguments themselves. Moreover, you can omit `const` and the reference specifications in the arguments; the metaobject compiler strips them anyway.
- Check the parameters of the signal and slot and ensure that they match *precisely*.
- Check to be sure that you've correctly declared the signal and slot portions of your header correctly.
- For that matter, be sure that your sender and receiver both inherit from `QObject` and that you have `Q_OBJECT` declared in your class definition. Remember, you need to do both.
- If you've forgotten part of the `QObject` declaration in your header, rerun `qmake` and rebuild.
- Make sure that you make the connection with `connect` before you invoke any functions that fire the signal.
- Make sure that you're not disconnecting the signal anywhere with `disconnect`.

Usually, the problem is pretty easy to track down, especially if you check the log and the signal and slot declarations closely. A common mistake is to wire a signal to a slot that's not been declared a slot, so check your headers closely!

Another thing to note: are your signals not disconnecting when they should? Consider the following line:

```
disconnect(object);
```

The preceding line is *not* the same as the following:

```
disconnect(object, 0, 0, 0);
```

This makes perfect sense when you look at the overloaded function definitions for `disconnect`, which read:

```
bool QObject::disconnect ( const QObject * receiver, const char *
method = 0 ).
```

Calling `disconnect` and passing only an object disconnects all the signals, rather than just the signal that you choose.

Summary

Qt and Qt Creator provide a great environment for application development, irrespective of whether you're writing console, GUI, or Qt Quick applications. You can mix and match standard C++ code with Qt, making the most of your existing skills. When doing this, you can add in things such as version control and command-line builds to your tools, giving you the ability to work in large teams and perform unattended builds of large projects using Qt. Qt has great documentation too, both bundled with Qt Creator and on the Web. With what you've learned in this book and what's available, the sky's the limit for your application development goals!

Index

Symbols

.pro file 29
QSizePolicy
  QSizePolicy::Minimum 108

A

active property, sensors 181
Ant
  URL 217
application
  debugging 44
  localized strings, including 198, 199
  localizing 194
  localizing, QLinguist used 196-198
  resources, using 57, 58
  running 44
audio clips
  playing 170-172
Audio type, properties
  autoLoad 172
  autoPlay 172
  bufferProgress 172
  duration 172
  error 172
  errorString 172
  hasAudio 172
  hasVideo 172
  loops 172
  muted 172
  position 172
  seekable 172
  volume 172
autosuggest 26

B

bearer network configuration
  URL 92
breakpoints
  setting 37, 38
Build menu 28

C

C++
  integrating, with Qt Quick 154-156
call stack
  examining 41, 42
camera
  accessing 175-177
Camera type, properties
  exposure 176
  flash 176
  focus 176
  imageCapture 175
  imageProcessing 176
  videoRecording 175
coding format options
  configuring 230, 231
coding style options
  configuring 230, 231
command line
  projects, building from 232
concrete model subclass
  analyzing 111-113
console applications
  writing, with Qt Creator 225-227
controller 109

currencies

localizing, QLocale used 199, 200

custom widgets

creating 123-126

D

data

representing, Qt's core classes used 80-82

dataRate property, sensors 181

dates

localizing, QLocale used 199, 200

debugging

for Windows, URL 35

device

location, determining 182-185

position, obtaining 186-191

dialogs

in application, instantiating 58-62

Digia 8

document object model (DOM) 68

drawing

off screen 122, 123

with QPainter, on QPaintDevice

instances 118-121

with Qt 118

E

environment variable

URL 218

event-driven programming 48

event model 48

Expression Evaluator 39

F

files

accessing, Qt used 86-89

files and network IO documentation

URL 89

forms

creating, in Qt Designer 52

instantiating 58-62

main form, creating 52-57

forward geodetic problem 184

G

Global Positioning System (GPS) 182

Graphics View Framework

about 127-136

URL 136

H

Hello World application

about 11, 12

QtGui library used 13-16

Qt Quick used 17-20

Hyper Text Transfer Protocol (HTTP)

about 89, 214

XML parsing used 93, 94

requests, performing 91

resources accessing, Qt used 89, 90

I

image gallery application

creating 156-166

input masks

character classes 106, 107

Internet Protocol (IP) 182

J

Java Development Kit (JDK) 217

K

key-value pairs

clear 83

empty 83

insert 83

key 83

keys 83

remove 83

working with 82, 83

L

landscape

learning 27-29

localization
about 193, 194
QLinguist used 196-198
strings, marking 195
localized strings
including, in application 198, 199
Long Term Evolution (LTE) 214
lost and found again
getting 35-37
low-level networking
URL

M

Makefile
URL 28
memory
examining 39-41
leaks finding, Valgrind used 206, 207
message boxes
instantiating 58-62
mobile application, testing 216
mobile platforms
supporting 223
mobile software development
about 212
computational resources 213
device considerations 212
mobile application, testing 216
network resources 214
storage resources 215
UI porting 215
user attention 212
user attention, key consequences 212
model 109
model-view-controller (MVC)
programming, with Qt 109-111
model/view pattern
URL 113
multimedia, Qt Quick
about 169, 170
using 169
multithreading
in Qt 84-86

N

Native Development Kit (NDK) 217
networking
URL 92
network samples
URL 92
Noun Project
URL 57

O

objects, QML
Drag 145
DropArea 146
Flickable 145
KeyNavigation 145
Keys 145
MouseArea 145
MultiPointTouchArea 145
PinchArea 145
TextEdit 146
TextInput 146
off screen
drawing 122, 123
onReadingChanged property, sensors 181
open method
QIODevice::Append 86
QIODevice::ReadOnly 86
QIODevice::ReadWrite 86
QIODevice::Text 87
QIODevice::Truncate 87
QIODevice::Unbuffered 87
QIODevice::WriteOnly 86

P

positioning elements, Qt Quick
Column 143
Flow 143
Grid 143
Row 143
PositionSource type, properties
active 182

name 182
preferredPositioningMethods 182
sourceError 183
supportedPositioningMethods 183
updateInterval 183
valid 183
Position type, properties
altitudeValid 183
coordinate 183
directionValid 183
horizontalAccuracy 183
horizontalAccuracyValid 183
latitudeValid 184
longitudeValid 184
speed 184
speedValid 184
timestamp 184
verticalAccuracy 184
verticalAccuracyValid 184
verticalSpeed 184
verticalSpeedValid 184
preferredPositioningMethods,
  PositionSource type
PositionSource.AllPositioningMethods 183
PositionSource.NonSatellite
  PositioningMethods 182
PositionSource.NoPositioningMethods 182
PositionSource.Satellite
  PositioningMethods 182
project
building, from command line 232
building 43
Projects pane 42, 43
Publish option 28

Q

QAbstractButton, properties
checkable 103
checked 103
down 103
icon 103
shortcut 103
text 103

QAbstractItemModel 110
QAbstractListModel 111
QAbstractTableModel 111
QAction class
about 101
enabled property 101
font property 101
icon property 101
iconVisibleInMenu property 101
shortcut property 101
text property 101
toolTip property 101
visible property 101
QByteArray 83
qDebug() 32
QFileSystemModel 111
QGraphicsEllipseItem 127
QGraphicsItem 127
QGraphicsRectItem 127
QGraphicsTextItem 127
QGuiApplication
applicationStateChanged signal 100
lastWindowClosed signal 100
QHash 82
QLineEdit, properties
alignment 105
cursorPosition 105
cursorPositionChanged 105
displayText 105
echoMode 105
editingFinished 105
hasSelectedText 105
inputMask 105
maxLength 105
placeholderText 105
readOnly 105
returnPressed 105
selectedText 105
selectionChanged 106
text 105
textChanged 106
textEdited 106
QLinguist
used, for localizing application 196-198

QList<T>::const iterator 82
QList<T>::iterator 82
QList<T> methods
  append 81
  at 81
  clear 81
  contains 81
  count 81
  empty 81
  endsWith 81
  first 81
  indexOf 81
  last 81
  lastIndexOf 81
  length 81
  prepend 81
  push_back 81
  push_front 81
  removeAt 81
  removeFirst 81
  removeLast 81
  replace 81
  startsWith 81
  swap 81
  toStdList 81
  toVector 81
QListView 110
QLocale
  currencies with 199, 200
  dates with 199, 200
qmake
  URL 29
QMap 82
QMenu, methods
  addAction 101
  addMenu 101
  addSeparator 101
  clear 101
  removeAction 101
QML
  and Qt Quick 77
  and Qt Quick, code interlude 67-69
  URL 69

QML performance analyzer 202
QML Profiler
  tabs 205
QMultiHash 82
QMultiMap 82
QMutex class
  lock method 85
  unlock method 85
QNetworkAccessManager class 91
QPaintDevice instances
  QPainter, drawing with 118-122
QPaintDevice, subclasses
  QBitmap 119
  QImage 118
  QPicture 119
  QPixmap 118
  QWidget 118
QPainter
  backgroundMode 119
  drawing with, on QPaintDevice
        instances 118-121
  brush 119
  font 119
  pen 119
QPainter, methods
  drawArc 120
  drawConvexPolygon 120
  drawEllipse 120
  drawImage 120
  drawLine 120
  drawPicture 120
  drawPixmap 121
  drawPoint and drawPoints 121
  drawPolygon 121
  drawPolyline 121
  drawRect 121
  drawText 121
  fillPath 121
  fillRect 121
QPicture 123
QSemaphore 86
QSizePolicy
  QSizePolicy::Expanding 108

QSizePolicy::Fixed 108
QSizePolicy::Maximum 108
QSizePolicy::MinimumExpanding 108
QSizePolicy::Preferred 108
QSqlQueryModel 111
QSqlRelationalTableModel 111
QSqlTableModel 111
QStandardItemModel 111
QStandardPaths::StandardLocation
  CacheLocation 89
  ConfigLocation 89
  DataLocation 88
  DesktopLocation 88
  DocumentsLocation 88
  HomeLocation 88
  MusicLocation 88
  PicturesLocation 88
  TempLocation 88
QString 83
QString, helper methods
  append 80
  arg 80
  at and operator[] 80
  clear 80
  contains 80
  count 80
  endsWith 80
  indexOf 80
  insert 80
  lastIndexOf 80
  length 80
  remove 80
  setNum 80
  split 80
  startsWith 80
  toDouble 80
  toFloat 80
  toInt 80
  toLong 80
  toLower 80
  toUpper 80
  truncate 80
QStringListModel 111

Qt
  about 7, 47, 79
  core classes, used for
    representing data 80-82
  documentation, URL 111
  downloading 8, 9
  drawing with 118
  menu sample, URL 103
  model-view-controller,
    programming with 109-111
  multithreading 84-86
  sensors 179, 180
  sensors, URL 181
  URL 8
  used, for accessing files 86-89
  used, for accessing HTTP resources 89, 90
  used, for parsing XML 92, 93
QTableView 110
Qt Assistant 235, 236
Qt C++ application
  QtLeakyButton 207-210
Qt Concurrent
  URL 86
Qt core container classes
  URL 83
Qt Creator
  about 7, 211, 235, 236
  configuring 220-222
  downloading 8, 9
  for Android, creating 217
  help documentation, URL 100
  integrating, with version
    control systems 227-229
  mobile platforms, supporting 223
  signal-slot connections, debugging 237
  URL 8, 223
  used, for writing console
    applications 225-227
  way, finding around 10, 11
Qt Creator class, features
  iteration 226
  memory performance 226
  portability 226
  readability 226

Qt Creator Designer
  QBoxLayout 107
  QFormLayout 107
  QGridLayout 107
  QHBoxLayout 107
  QStackedLayout 107
  QVBoxLayout 107
Qt Creator, for Android
  creating 217
  environment variables, setting 218
  Qt Quick Hello World, building 223
  Qt Quick Hello World, running 223
  requisites, downloading 217
  SDK installation, finishing 219, 220
Qt Creator, variables
  CONFIG 29
  HEADERS 29
  INSTALLS 29
  QT 29
  SOURCES 29
  TARGET 29
  TEMPLATE 29
Qt Designer
  forms, creating in 52
  Qt Quick applications, creating 70, 71
Qt documentation
  URL 35
QtGui library
  used, for Hello World application 13-16
QThread
  about 84
  URL 86
QtLeakyButton 207-209
Qt Linguist 193
Qt Meta-object Language (QML) 33, 47, 139
Qt Multimedia
  URL 170
QtPositioning module
  Coordinate 182
  Position 182
  PositionSource 182
Qt Project forums
  URL 236

Qt Quick
  about 139
  and QML 77
  and QML syntax 67-69
  fundamental concepts 139-149
  integrating, with C++ 154-156
  mobile application performance,
    enhancing 213
  multimedia 169
  states 149-153
  transitions 149-153
  used, for Hello World application 17-20
  window display options, setting 233-235
Qt Quick application
  calculator's main view 74-76
  creating, in QT Designer 70, 71
  reusable Button, creating 71-73
  QtSlowButton 202-206
Qt Quick Hello World application
  building 223
  running 223
QTreeView 110
QtSlowButton 202-206
Qt::Window flags
  Qt::Desktop 233
  Qt::FramelessWindowHint 233
  Qt::Popup 233
  Qt::WindowStaysOnBottomHint 233
  Qt::WindowStaysOnTopHint 233
QWebPage, signals
  initialLayoutCompleted 114
  loadFinished 114
  loadStarted 114
  pageChanged 114
  urlChanged 114
QWebView
  loadFinished 114
  loadProgress 114
  loadStarted 114
  web content, rendering with 113-115
QWebView, properties
  hasSelection 114
  icon 114
  selectedHtml 114

selectedText 114
title 114
url 114
zoomFactor 114
QWidget
about 66, 100-105
application logic, wiring 63-66
documentation, URL 126
QXmlStreamReader class
URL 92

R

readNext
Characters 93
Comment 93
DTD 93
EndDocument 93
EndElement 93
EntityReference 93
ProcessingInstruction 93
StartDocument 93
StartElement 93
reusable Button
creating 71-73
reverse geodetic problem 184
roleNames method 166

S

sample library
about 23, 24
creating 25, 27
linking against 30-35
sensors
in Qt 179-181
sensors, properties
active 181
dataRate 181
onReadingChanged 181
setRootPath method 166
signals 48-51
signal-slot connections, Qt Creator
debugging 237
signals, MouseArea
onClicked 146

onDoubleClicked 146
onEntered 146
onExited 146
onPressed 146
onReleased 146
onWheel 146
slots 48-52
Software Development Kit (SDK) 217
sound effects
playing 170-172
SoundEffect type
fields 171
special parameters
localizing, QLocale used 199
Standard Template Library (STL) 226
states, Qt Quick 149-153
strings
marking, for localization 195

T

The Noun Project
URL 212
toString method
QLocale::LongFormat 200
QLocale::NarrowFormat 200
QLocale::ShortFormat 200
transitions, Qt Quick 150-153

V

Valgrind
about 207
URL 207
used, for finding memory leaks 206, 207
variables
examining 39
version control systems
about 227
Qt Creator, integrating with 227-229
video clips
playing 173, 174
VideoOutput, properties
autoOrientation 174
contentRect 174
fillMode 175

  orientation 175
  sourceRect 175
view 109
visual elements, Qt Quick
  AnimatedImage 144
  AnimatedSprite 144
  Image 144
  Item 144
  Text 144
  Window 144

W

web content
  rendering with 113, 114
WebKit browser
  URL 115
widget layout
  managing, with layouts 107-109
  URL 109
window display options, Qt Quick
  setting 233-235
WorkerThread
  implementing 95, 97

X

XML
  parsing, HTTP used 93, 94
  parsing, Qt used 92, 93

Thank you for buying
Application Development with Qt Creator
Second Edition

About Packt Publishing

Packt, pronounced 'packed', published its first book "*Mastering phpMyAdmin for Effective MySQL Management*" in April 2004 and subsequently continued to specialize in publishing highly focused books on specific technologies and solutions.

Our books and publications share the experiences of your fellow IT professionals in adapting and customizing today's systems, applications, and frameworks. Our solution based books give you the knowledge and power to customize the software and technologies you're using to get the job done. Packt books are more specific and less general than the IT books you have seen in the past. Our unique business model allows us to bring you more focused information, giving you more of what you need to know, and less of what you don't.

Packt is a modern, yet unique publishing company, which focuses on producing quality, cutting-edge books for communities of developers, administrators, and newbies alike. For more information, please visit our website: www.packtpub.com.

About Packt Open Source

In 2010, Packt launched two new brands, Packt Open Source and Packt Enterprise, in order to continue its focus on specialization. This book is part of the Packt Open Source brand, home to books published on software built around Open Source licenses, and offering information to anybody from advanced developers to budding web designers. The Open Source brand also runs Packt's Open Source Royalty Scheme, by which Packt gives a royalty to each Open Source project about whose software a book is sold.

Writing for Packt

We welcome all inquiries from people who are interested in authoring. Book proposals should be sent to author@packtpub.com. If your book idea is still at an early stage and you would like to discuss it first before writing a formal book proposal, contact us; one of our commissioning editors will get in touch with you.

We're not just looking for published authors; if you have strong technical skills but no writing experience, our experienced editors can help you develop a writing career, or simply get some additional reward for your expertise.

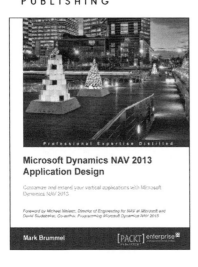
Microsoft Dynamics NAV 2013 Application Design

ISBN: 978-1-78217-036-5   Paperback: 504 pages

Customize and extend your vertical applications with Microsoft Dynamics NAV 2013

1. Set up your application for a number of vertical industries and scenarios.

2. Get acquainted with Dynamics NAV's data model and transaction schema with the help of highly efficient design patterns.

3. Consists of two completely designed and explained vertical solutions, including application objects.

Application Development in iOS 7

ISBN: 978-1-78355-031-9   Paperback: 126 pages

Learn how to build an entire real-world application using all of iOS 7's new features

1. Get acquainted with the new features of iOS 7 through real-world, project-based learning.

2. Take an in-depth look at Xcode 5, Foundation, and autolayout.

3. Utilize the full source code and assets present to build an actual interactive application.

Please check **www.PacktPub.com** for information on our titles

Made in the USA
San Bernardino, CA
21 March 2017